Will your
PRODIGAL
come Home?

an honest
discussion of
struggle & hope

Will your
PRODIGAL
come Home?

JEFF LUCAS

ZONDERVAN®

ZONDERVAN.com/
AUTHORTRACKER
follow your favorite authors

ZONDERVAN®

Will Your Prodigal Come Home?
Copyright © 2007 by Jeff Lucas

Requests for information should be addressed to:

Zondervan, Grand Rapids, Michigan 49530

Library of Congress Cataloging-in-Publication Data

Lucas, Jeff, 1956 –
    Will your prodigal come home? : an honest discussion of struggle & hope /
Jeff Lucas.
      p. cm.
    Includes bibliographical references.
    ISBN-13: 978-0-310-26725-6
    ISBN-10: 0-310-26725-0
1. Parenting – Religious aspects – Christianity. 2. Parent and teenager – Religious
aspects – Christianity. 3. Problem youth – Family relationships. 4. Ex-church
members – Family relationships. I. Title.
    BV4529.L84   2006
    248.8'45 – dc22

                         2006033913

Poem on pages 184 – 85 reprinted with permission.

Interior design by Beth Shagene

Printed in the United States of America

07 08 09 10 11 12 • 22 21 20 19 18 17 16 15 14 13 12 11 10 9 8 7 6 5 4 3 2 1

To all who wait for a better day
and a party to come.

Contents

Acknowledgments

My thanks to Rob Parsons, Jonathan Booth, Amy Boucher-Pye, John Sloan, Dary Northrop, Steve, Sherri, and Craig Harris, and the dynamic Zondervan team in Grand Rapids. And Kay, thank you for every day.

chapter one

A Familiar Story

Sherri and Steve heard their son frantically gasping for air before they saw him.

Craig's labored rasping greeted them as they stepped into their house. They had headed home from church with that warm glow of accomplishment and gratitude that pastors feel following a "good" Sunday morning service. A barbeque and a lazy afternoon was the plan. All that changed as they opened the door.

Craig lay sprawled on the couch, his puffy face a pallid gray, save for the alarming rash on his cheek. Clawing at a cushion, he fought desperately for breath. His immune system was shutting down quickly, short-circuited by last night's lethal cocktail of crystal methadone and crack cocaine. His eyes were wide with fear and brimming with tears.

Paralyzed, Sherri and Steve stared at their darling son as he writhed in pain before them. After a stunned moment, they began trying to save his life. Sherri grabbed the phone and called for medical help; Steve tried to keep hold of Craig's clammy hands as he thrashed around, as if by catching hold of him he could save him from plunging into the abyss.

This was yet another painful junction on the long and unanticipated road they had trekked for four years. As a child,

Craig had always been enthusiastic about God and the church. He was tenderhearted, often weeping when he prayed, and keen that his friends would know Christ. Inheriting his parents' love of music, he had joined the worship team and was a fine vocalist. Then, overnight, or so it seemed to his parents, everything changed.

To Sherri and Steve, it appeared that a dark Jekyll-and-Hyde transformation was happening to their son, an evil takeover bid that they were powerless to prevent. There was no trauma they knew of that signaled Craig's decision to so dramatically change his life. There were no conversations or questions that signaled the gathering of dark storm clouds, no hints that could help them to steel themselves for what was to come. Craig's first experience of drugs was like a dark conversion, sudden and cataclysmic. It was the beginning of the family's nightmare.

Craig would often return home in the middle of the night stupefied into a drug- and alcohol-fueled delirium, cursing loudly and screaming at his sisters. And then there were the nights—and the weeks—when he didn't come home at all and didn't call. Sleepless, Sherri and Steve would stare through the gloom at their bedroom ceiling and wonder if their son was alive or dead. As they lay there, the sound of every passing car would birth hope and then, when it was not him, shroud them with disappointment. The scraping of his key in the door would give momentary joy and relief, which was then dashed when they saw the terrible state he was in. They would have to undress him and put him in bed, just as when he was a child. But these days, he would be spattered with his own vomit, and he interspersed terrible curses with tender, apologetic words, and then whimpered curses again as he drifted in and out of delirium. Finally, he would sleep, sometimes for fifteen hours. The next day, they would hear him in the shower, and then, without so much as a good-bye, the door of their home would slam behind him once more. Sherri would hurry into his bedroom and place her hand on the still-warm bedsheet.

Every Christian Knows a Prodigal

Sherri and Steve's experience was extreme. A prodigal— someone who walks away from intimacy with God—doesn't always become a drug or alcohol abuser, or a star player on the party circuit. But probably every Christian on earth knows and grieves for someone whose life choices make a bleak declaration: the good news of the gospel has not been good enough for them.

At every level of society today, in the plain homes of the poor and in the glitzy mansions of the rich, in black and white and yellow and brown families, tears will flow as children, partners, parents, siblings, or friends head away from God, and in some cases, walk away from us too. Close relationships will fragment; once-happy families will be shattered as prodigals drift or stomp off. Doors will be slammed and words will be hurled around in haste, verbal missiles that will long be regretted but can never be called back. It will happen to people who hail from every denomination and style of church; there's no religious outfit that is prodigal-proof. Prodigals come from seeker-sensitive as well as hot-gospeling churches; from renewed, Spirit-filled congregations as well as those whose main priority is the exegetical preaching of Scripture; from dynamic churches that are connected with and serving their communities, as well as those who tend to retreat and hide from the big, bad world.

Whatever their background, for those left behind, every day becomes like living in a cold, drafty room in which a small fire of hope flickers against the chill, and then sometimes finally dies. And we never thought it could happen to us.

It's always such a shock when someone you dearly love morphs and walks. No one ever planned to raise a child who would toss God aside like the toys of infancy. When you held that fluffy, pink bundle in your arms and wept tears of thanksgiving to God for that precious gift, you never imagined the pain to come. Or when you prayed prayers of passion and commitment with that closest friend, and then shared your dreams together into the wee, small hours, you assumed that you—and they—would walk all of your days hand in hand with God. And then they changed their mind and gradually drifted from him, or perhaps they suddenly dumped him.

If you are a parent, perhaps you shook your head when you heard news of other people's children hiking the pigpen trail. I hope you never voiced your opinion that most likely deficient parenting was to blame. But then you looked at your growing, smiling children, so active in church, so in love with God, and you told yourself that this would never happen to *your* family. Like all bad things—cancer, bankruptcy, devastating car wrecks—all these and other tragedies were for others; surely they would not visit you. We're all hoping to live the sunny story line where everyone lives happily ever after. Until ...

But humans make accomplished drifters. The Bible doesn't spare our blushes. Sheep aren't noted for their brains and wisdom and are rather good at getting lost, and Scripture affirms that we're just like them.[1] No wonder that the parable of the prodigal that Jesus told is his most famous and familiar, for we can all identify with it so easily. Perhaps our ability to get lost comes as no surprise to us; what continues to be a wonderful, jolting shock is the way a loving God responds to our compulsively meandering ways. He longs for the prodigals to come home to his heart and is on the lookout for them at this very moment.

Waiting and Watching

The man stands where he always stands, quite alone. As the afternoon sun slowly dips into the horizon, he peers through the fading light. You will find him in that very spot every day; same time, same place.

His vantage point is at the eastern perimeter of the farm, where a long, rocky, uneven trail begins and snakes off toward the distant country. He studies that gently undulating pathway with the diligence of a sentry. Ramrod still, he barely breathes, so absolute is his concentration. It is as if he is nervous even to blink, lest in that split second of not seeing, he might miss what he so longs to see. He stares out into the gathering gloom, hating the darkness to come, knowing that out there the night spells danger. He prays while he looks, imagining that he is hurling great handfuls of divine power and protection out into the distance where they are so needed.

Like ten thousand times before, he hears a faint, familiar voice: *Abba*. It is the sound of a boy calling for his father. He turns his head to listen. But the wind is mocking him, whispering through a nearby shrub; that is all it is.

That is all it is.

He moves his focus a little to the left and scans the horizon once more. Somewhere out there is his son, he hopes. That is why he comes here, every day without fail. To not come would be to bow to his greatest fear: that his boy is dead already. It is getting darker by the second, and he shivers in the chill. Finally he turns and struggles uphill toward the house that used to be such a warm home before that fateful day. His back is bowed down as if by a huge burden. Tomorrow the old man will be back at his appointed place, watching, waiting.

He loves one who has left. He loves a prodigal.

One of Our Most Beloved Stories Ever Told

The parable of the prodigal son is one of the oldest, best-loved stories in the world. It has all the winning components of a page-turning tale: heartbreak and trauma, five-star playboy living and then a freefall from riches to rags, jealousy exploding into rage, and a happy ending—but one with a twist. And it comes from one of the world's greatest storytellers.

In the parable of the lost son, a father of two sons unexpectedly finds he has only one. The youngest of the pair, seduced by the promise of forbidden pleasure, decides that he is done once and for all with the quiet life. The family farm is secure, but tedious. Safety often carries the price of predictability, and where he spends his grey days, there's little room for high-energy living. Home has become ho-hum, and work a joyless dirge. He could really use some fun. He wants a life.

At first he was just vaguely bored, but then boredom distilled into anger. And now the young son struggles to conceal a growing rage that simmers within and threatens to boil over. Frustrated, he grinds his teeth, mutters curses to no one in particular, and eyes the door with a prisoner's hunger for freedom.

But his impatience is starting to show. His father's endlessly repeated stories, once such a delight, are hackneyed and pathetic now. The young son, so much "wiser" and "more sophisticated" than his hobo family, doesn't snicker at those familiar punch lines anymore, even out of duty. A sneer lives where once there was a smile, and he flushes with embarrassment when Dad looks hopefully around the room, expecting a laugh at his worn-out comic routines. The young son stares woodenly at the floor, feet tapping furiously like the tail of an angry cat, eager to be excused from the table—and from this tiresome family. He and his father's eyes don't meet much at all these days; a good thing too, for then his father would know his contempt. Father and son both sleep very little, kept awake by what both know must surely come. Sad inevitability is in the air, but neither dares acknowledge it yet.

For the son, every waking moment is now spent daydreaming about being miles from his father's home, business, protection, values, and—most of all—far from his arms and the stifling control that they represent. The bright lights in the distance wink and beckon, never failing in their nightly call to him. The horizon seems bathed with an enchanting, irresistible allure. He sees himself surrounded by clever, witty, creative people—beautiful human beings, worldly wise and so very alive. Once his father seemed like such a seasoned life traveler; now he is just an ignorant yokel with his blinkered opinions and his narrow morality. What does he know about the real world anyway? His homespun sayings have never been tested beyond the fields. The son longs to know and to understand for himself.

And some of the surging undertow that threatens to sweep him off his feet is not so noble. In his fantasies, women, all willing and grinning and gorgeous, bustle around him offering their ready, soft flesh. At first, his flights of fancy prompted feelings of shame, but those days are long over; his imagination has roamed far and sunk deep. His skin hides the mind of one who longs to live amorally.

As for the father, he feels impotent, pathetic even. Once he was lord over the little kingdom of his farm. Now, as he sees his son looking down, looking at the ceiling, looking at his fingernails, looking at anything but him, he knows that a day of greater pain is very near and dreads its dawning.

The showdown erupts and the younger pounds the table, demanding his inheritance *now*, as if his father was already dead and buried. The parting of their ways is agonizing for the father; if the son realizes he has wounded by making his demand, he certainly doesn't show it. Blinded by selfishness, he is oblivious to the grief that clouds his dad's eyes. His bags are packed and bulging. And within days, he takes his body off to where his mind has lived for months.

The Far Country

Now he is just a distant dot on the horizon, striding resolutely toward a world of hurt, to pain beyond his dreams as he heads to a place known as "the far country." That term is largely meaningless to us and implies only that he took a lengthy trek. But to those who first heard Jesus' story, it was a turn of phrase pregnant with meaning. The Decapolis, a district of ten cities in northeast Galilee, was the Sodom and

Gomorrah of the day, a region that offered all the dirt and delights of a red-light district. Here was an erotic theater and even a version of the Olympic Games where the contestants competed naked. The Jews sniffed with disdain at the whole area and called it a pigsty, and it was in Gadera (one of the ten cities) where Jesus cast demons out of two men into a herd of swine.[2] So the prodigal ends up in the pig region, feeding on swine food—enough to make kosher hair stand on end. Jesus painted a vivid word picture of a good boy gone very, very bad—one down and very much out.

And so the son marches to a place that is very much like a movie set, where illusions reign and nothing is quite what it seems. The high life is real enough, and he hurls himself into days and nights where he goes wherever his hormones steer him. There is no shortage of grinning, good-time friends. But hours of heady exhilaration are punctuated by hollow, grey days. When lust is spent and the alcohol that beautifies too many plain partners wears off, he wakes with a splitting headache and a heavy heart, dissatisfied, and yet unwilling to admit his dissatisfaction.

He thought that his mind would clear in the far country, that life would finally make sense, but instead, a thick fog of confusion shrouds him. He and his bohemian friends talk endlessly about satisfaction, contentment, and discovering the ultimate reality—but behind all the high-sounding, pseudo-academic chatter, they all know the truth about each other's leanness of soul. Perhaps they pledge friendship forever; but the far country is stacked wall to wall with users, fair-weather pals who'll love you forever—or until your wallet is empty, whichever comes first.

So when the money runs out, his "friends" run too. And the good-time boy falls on hard times and ends up malnourished, lonely, and daydreaming yet again of better times he took for granted at home. He spends long days looking back over his shoulder at what used to be.

Meanwhile, back at the ranch, hearts break and slowly bleed. There is longing, regret, and wondering: Will their loved one ever return? And that's the question we're asking about the ones that we love, who right now are apparently putting distance between themselves and God. Perhaps we too were tossed aside in the fallout, no longer needed. Will our prodigals return home?

Why This Book?

When we discover that someone we love is tramping the war-path against God, with the first pit stop on the trail being the pigpen, we are left feeling desolate, sometimes hopeless, and very, very alone.

So let's pause for a while and huddle together for warmth. There are a few things about me and about this book that I'd like you to know. We're about to take a fairly intimate journey together, so let's get acquainted. Although I'm British, I spend most of my time in America as a teaching pastor at Timberline Church in Fort Collins, Colorado, a fast-growing, "prodigal-friendly" church. I'm intimately familiar with jet-lag, however, because I get back to the British Isles regularly for the ministry I still do there.

The idea for this book didn't begin with me. Rob Parsons is another British Christian leader, and a message of "Bringing Home the Prodigals" was birthed in his heart in 2002. He wrote a book under that title, and as a result has seen many thousands attending prayer and teaching events across the UK.

In Britain, the Prodigals message is more than just a book—it's a movement.

Rob recognized the need for a similar movement in North America and thus invited me to take the heartbeat of the Prodigals message and present it here. This book is the result.

Real Hope for the Journey

In the pages that follow, I want to bring hope that is substantial and real. I promise you no easy recipes for success, no surefire promises that will end up adding disappointment to the pain you already feel. Some of our prodigals will not come home, no matter how much we pray and long for their return. But most of us do not need to resign ourselves to that unhappy ending at this point in our stories. And we may never have to.

This book is for those who have children—of whatever age—who are prodigals. But it's not only for parents, because other relatives and friends of the prodigals also carry deep pain for loved ones who are living in the far country. In short, if your heart aches for a prodigal, this book is for you.

Together we'll ask how prodigals are made—and we'll consider the caution that some prodigals are not prodigals at all. Our grief has caused us to misunderstand them and hastily name them what they are not. And then we will ask why it is that some really do turn their backs on God. We owe it to our prodigals to ask some searching and sometimes painful questions. A survey was conducted called "Gone but Not Forgotten," and it revealed the scandal that nine out of ten of those who have left the church were never asked *why* they walked. Leslie Francis commented on our reluctance to ask the important question *why*: "It is an indictment that so many leavers said that no one seemed to notice they'd gone. That's careless."[3]

So we'll notice their leaving and wonder why they went. Then we'll consider our passionate God and the seemingly endless sagas of his wayward kids. It's important for us to focus on the Father. When Jesus introduced the key players in this famous drama, he listed the character of the father first. He told the story to shock his listeners with love— God's love. Faced by the persnickety mutterings of his religious critics, who were forever looking for a "better" class of sinner, Jesus painted a breathtaking portrait of a patient, selfless, generous, singing, dancing God. He threw back the curtain of eternity to show that there is a perfect parent at the heart of the universe, in sharp contrast to the practiced dullness and turgid orthodoxy of the Pharisees, represented in the story by the villain of the piece, the elder brother. The lead character in the story is neither the profligate son, nor the elder brother, but the father. When Rembrandt gave the world his masterpiece *The Return of the Prodigal Son* in 1669, he placed the father as the centerpiece and focal point of the painting. We only see the kneeling son from behind. And a figure that some identify as the elder brother stands watching from the right, a spectator only, not the center of attention. So we'll take a luxurious look at the Father who is eternally loving, yet endlessly frustrated.

We'll reflect on what it feels like to love and care about a prodigal, and to realize that our pain is shared by many. We'll ask some awkward questions about what "coming home" might actually mean. We'll consider just why we should be hopeful, without resorting to clichés or slogans. And we'll identify a force that hijacks our prayers and eclipses our best days—false guilt. We'll consider how we can best pray, and ponder what it means to prepare a party of outrageous grace that will be so colorful and generous, so vital and vibrant, that it stuns the prodigal, shocks the elder brother, and makes the far country parties seem pathetic and paltry by comparison. We'll plan parties that will make angels skip and Pharisees stamp their feet in indignant rage. We'll think about catering an over-the-top bash that is totally undeserved, unexpected, and unparalleled in extravagance.

We'll see that when there's a homecoming, the journey hasn't ended—it's just continuing.

As we journey together, I won't assault you with dozens of real-life anecdotes—just a few will suffice. And I won't ask you to wade through statistics about prodigality; the fact that you hold this book in your hands means that you probably have your own story of a parting of the ways, and that is enough.

Can I ask that we pause before we move forward? Let's remember that we are not talking about a faceless somebody generically known as "a prodigal." Most of you know from experience that we are not talking about faceless somebodies, but much-loved individuals who are precious to us. But for those who don't know a prodigal, remember that they are not just anonymous case histories. In Francis Ford Coppola's movie *The Conversation*, a couple passes by a homeless man sleeping on a park bench, and the woman ponders the prone, unmoving man and sees more than a pile of rags. "He was once somebody's baby boy," she says. As we share these reflections together, we are thinking and praying, not about a "problem segment of the church," but about the hopes, tears, and fears of genuine human beings, each of them the unique poetry of God, each one priceless in his sight. And for those whose hearts break, we are considering your nearest and dearest who perhaps right now are a very long way away, and so I promise to tread carefully. Perhaps we will share some smiles as well as tears. I hope so.

Please walk slowly and quietly through these pages. As we journey together, let's pause at times to bring our prodigals to the cross of Christ. There we find the mingling of our own utter helplessness and God's total power to intervene and save. There is no better place to go—for us, or for the prodigals we weep for.

So join me now as we do what many whose hearts are broken for prodigals rarely do.

Let's talk.

chapter two

Cruel School

Suffering, once accepted, loses its edge,
for the terror of it lessens, and what remains is generally
far more manageable than we had imagined.
LESLEY HAZELTON

They called it "the tribulation," and it was a particularly fiendish form of execution that the ancient Greeks used. Give me the hangman's noose, the gas chamber, or even the diabolical electric chair rather than this. Death came by gradual, never-ending crushing. A huge rock was placed upon the chest of a condemned prisoner, and he would be left alone, helpless and hopeless. Over a period of days, the weight would literally crush the life out of him, snapping his bones and finally compressing his chest cavity, until his thousands of small breaths mercifully stopped. The poetic King James Version uses the word *tribulation* to describe the pressure that followers of Jesus often experience.[1] Those whose hearts have been broken by prodigals begin each day with the realization of the rock still upon their chest. There are some cold, dark mornings when they can hardly get out of bed, overwhelmed at the thought of carrying the burden for yet another day. At times nothing is felt but the weight of that rock. Joy is eclipsed by it, as are blue skies and heaven. Indeed, heaven itself seems a long way off. This pain is the price we pay for loving; it's the hurt that comes from being stabbed by razor-sharp words, from the dull ache of ongoing rejection, and from the heaviness that comes from living in fear and dread. And it is suffering that comes to us as a direct consequence of being a follower and friend of Christ. Without him set daily as our purpose and priority, we would not be concerned about others being far from the Father's house, for we would not be there ourselves. Only those who follow can weep for those who follow no more.

But it is the price worth paying, and the pain worth facing. C. S. Lewis says:

> Love anything, and your heart will be wrung and possibly broken. If you want to make sure of keeping it intact you must give it to no one, not even an animal. Wrap it carefully round with hobbies and little luxuries; avoid all entanglements. Lock it up safe in a casket or coffin of your selfishness. But in that casket—safe, dark, motionless, airless—it will change. It will not be broken; it will become unbreakable, impenetrable, irredeemable. To love is to be vulnerable.[2]

No one in her right mind welcomes pain or even wants to give it the time of day. All of us live, to some degree, in fear of losing what's most dear to us. And fear often triumphs because it stalks in the fog of the unknown. So when we squarely face the struggle of what might be involved in loving a prodigal, we do so not to depress ourselves, but to square our jaws for the journey and to seek God's strength for the day. Sherri and Steve's journey has a single lesson for us all: to be the parent of a prodigal is to experience the cruelest of educations. God promises his company with us on that shadowy road, but that does not negate the fact that the road is still dark, and the long, uphill climb exhausting.

The Eyes Have It

Sherri longed for the good old days, when cell phones still sounded vaguely like telephones. The dreadful advent of downloadable ring tones now meant that callers announced themselves with orchestral strings, torrential rainfall, the crying of a baby, or—worst of all—the monotonous thudding of gangster rap. As Craig's phone exploded into life for the fifth time that hour, Sherri realized how much she loathed that ring tone: it signaled another interruption into the precious little time that she had with her son. Couldn't those friends of his leave him alone for just an hour or two? They'd already stolen him away, or so Sherri felt, and they had so much time with him. Why couldn't he turn off the wretched phone?

And then she resented what happened to Craig as he answered every call with the same words. "Hey—what's up?" The surly, noncommunicative young man with whom she was struggling to have a conversation, this son of hers who insisted on watching football even while they "talked," suddenly became animated and interested when he answered that phone. And sometimes, even while she was trying so hard to chat with him, his thumb would move across the phone keys at lightning speed as he chatted with yet more friends through text, while occasionally nodding and grunting at her. She felt like a distraction. As he chattered in the phone about hot plans for that night and focused on a touchdown on television, she took a long look at him.

Craig looked rough. These days he never bothered with an iron, so his clothes were creased, his white shirts grey, almost matching his pallid skin. Unshaven whiskers sprouted here and there on his cheeks, resilient against a hasty shave. The rare hugs that Sherri shared with her son were always stained by the smell of nicotine.

But what alarmed her more were his eyes. As usual, they were bloodshot (she hoped from too little sleep rather than drugs), his eyelids puffy. His eyes seemed dull, clouded; once they had been soft, wide open with wonder, sparkling warmth when he flashed that dazzling—and now all-too-rare—smile.

Now they were narrow slits, at times cynical, mocking even. To see Craig with his eyes wide open was unusual these days. She couldn't help but look during a family meal when a prayer of thanks was offered. Craig sat back in his chair and stared straight ahead, as if to close his eyes for even the briefest moment of prayer would have been too compliant. The wooden expression on his face spoke volumes: this was a silent protest against the God he had abandoned. Before his family at least, he and God were apparently no longer on speaking terms. Or was Sherri just reading too much into the simple fact that Craig didn't choose to close his eyes?

Sherri closed the dishwasher and waited for Craig to end his call. He flipped his phone shut and punched the mute button on the television, the commentator's voice once again filling the room, the volume just a little too loud.

Was Craig avoiding conversation, bored or irritated by her chattering? Was there something dreadful that he wanted to keep from her, and did he fear that conversation might unearth it? Or perhaps he was just enjoying the football game …

God only knew. And he wasn't saying.

Daydreams and Nightmares

For parents who have prodigals in the far country, ordinary daily happenings become fearsome ogres. A telephone ringing in the middle of the night is never a welcome sound for anyone, but it instantly transports the parent of a prodigal. In that heart-stopping moment of blinking awake, you stare at the glowing LED of your alarm clock, *3:12 a.m.*, and fumble for the phone. In that second, you—in your mind's eye, at least—are standing before an open casket that holds the broken body of your child. Or you find yourself on a remote road next to a wrecked, bloodied car, bathed in the flashing lights of an ambulance. You develop a stunning ability to imagine the worst. You sweat and sometimes tremble as your mind, like a mad computer out of control, skips through any number of horrifying fates that might befall your prodigal. You used to sit back, sip coffee, and daydream about bright and beautiful things ahead for them. Now you can only fear the darkness to come. And it's not just the thought of a bleak future that terrifies you: the here and now is bad enough.

Sleep often eludes you, and the shadows and stillness of the night magnify your fears. You toss and turn and punch pillows in vain because your mind just refuses to shut down. You may suffer panic attacks, feeling that you are drowning or being buried alive or being suffocated by the darkness of your room. At times, staying in bed is impossible. You get up, perhaps go to another part of the house and turn on a light. It helps a little. In that bleak place called the small hours, you might go into your son or daughter's bedroom, just in case they might have soundlessly slipped into the house. As you open the door, hope and dreadful fear collide. They might be there, alive and well. And where there is a fear of suicide or drug overdose, they might be there, cold and lifeless.

When sleep finally comes, peace does not always come with it. Your rest might be ravaged by fearful nightmares—sometimes you wonder if they contain messages from God—and then you wake exhausted to realize that your journey cannot be left behind in a dream. The new dawn offers no relief. You haul yourself reluctantly into another day, shaky and nauseated because of the lack of sleep, and fearful that today's reality might be worse than last night's terrible dream. You live with a lingering sense of dread that mugs you just when you're relaxed or having a little fun.

You cry easily and without warning. A movie about happy family life at first warms your heart, then taunts you; tears flow as onscreen laughter and hugs are shared. And being around real-life, happy households makes you feel your own failures more acutely. Their well-being heightens your sense of wretchedness. You covet what they have, who they are. You'd quite like to live their life. Most of the time you don't wish your struggles on them, but you wouldn't mind their life exchanged for yours. Why did you get the short straw? How would they cope with the bitterness that you taste every day with your prodigal?

"Well-Meaning" Friends

Sherri and Steve became irritated at first, and then angered by trite clichés and slogans from their friends. The prattle grew familiar as people trotted out their meaningless mantras. Perhaps those who "shared" their nifty little slogans had previous experience—as counselors to an unfortunate chap called Job.

"He's a good kid, really." *Right now, he's pretty skilled at being bad.*

"He'll get there in the end." *Yeah. Hopefully before we're dead.*

"When it gets really bad, pray through." *Wonderful. Why not join us for a prayer meeting at three a.m.? Our kid on crack cocaine might be conscious enough to join us and say an amen.*

"When the going gets tough, the tough get going." *Thank you. Perhaps you'd like to get going yourself now.*

They wanted to gather up all the careless comments, throw them into a basket, and burn the basket. With attitude.

Some other well-meaning friends unwittingly wounded them, taking upon themselves the mantle, but not the gifting, of a prophet. They assured Sherri and Steve that it was all going to be alright and that the kid would turn out fine. How could they know what the future held? Had some angel told them as spectators on the sidelines what Sherri and Steve didn't know as suffering parents? The promises started to sound like pledges from a fairground huckster: loud, generic, and hollow. Worst of all was the frequent statement, "I know how you feel." Even with those who are fellow sufferers with prodigals of their own, "I know how you feel" is limited. What did their friends know about living for weeks not knowing whether your son is dead or alive? How could they know what it felt like to be treated by the police as guilty by association when they called to say that he had been arrested? The curt manner of some law enforcement officers made them feel small, as if the parents of someone who has been arrested should be indicted for conceiving them. What did those who "knew how they felt" know about taking a call from that acid-tongued woman from the debt collection agency? She spends her days threatening and harassing, and now sharply demands that you take a message and makes no attempt to disguise her contempt, as if you were the one who wrote that bad check. Do those who "know how you feel" know how that little conversation made you feel?

And when meeting with fellow leaders who knew about Craig, Steve and Sherri wondered what they *really* thought about them and their wayward boy. Behind the smiles and the encouragement, did their colleagues quietly think that not only were they deficient parents, but that their home situation disqualified them from leadership? Would a day come when Steve would lose his job as well as his son?

It was also difficult when other parents shared about their kids' grades and their spiritual aspirations. Sherri and Steve would smile and genuinely try to be glad. But it hurt. Never once did they wish their own pain on anyone else, yet the light in the eyes of the others made their own darkness feel ever bleaker.

Nudged into Isolation

You learn to steel yourself for certain times of the year. Thanksgiving hurts. The empty chair at the family table silently reminds throughout the meal that someone is missing. They might have promised to be there, but never made it and didn't call to offer an explanation. Your family prayer of gratitude included a few extra lines, asking for protection and grace for an absent daughter. You quickly wiped away a few tears as you carved the turkey.

Christmas might be worse. It hurts shopping for a gift, knowing that your child might not be home to open it, and that probably no gift will be reciprocated. Little children bustling around at church, woodenly reciting their lines in the nativity play, remind you of the wonderful moment when, at age five, your child had played the part of the innkeeper and opened the door to Joseph and Mary, who were begging for a place to rest. He forgot his lines, decided to make up some of his own, and told Mary and Joseph that there was plenty of room in the inn, thus rewriting the whole nativity story in a moment. The congregation was delighted. You remember, laugh out loud, and cry out loud.

For Sherri and Steve, the situation relentlessly nudged them into isolation. When people asked how Craig was doing, they found themselves fumbling for answers, not wanting to lie and yet not wanting to expose him. "He's fine," they would reply. Of course, he was anything but fine. He wasn't around because he was in jail. The last time they saw him, he was in a devastating valley following a meth high. The last call they'd taken for him was from the police, who were eager to get acquainted again with their son. But no one wants to give such a report, and they knew that some wouldn't want to hear it anyway. They feared that they had worn out even their closest friends and family members by talking too much about Craig's situation, that what everybody really wanted was for Craig to be fine, if for no other reason than that they could then move on and talk of happier things.

Sherri and Steve remained fiercely protective of their son. One day, Craig, filthy, stinking, and looking a wreck, decided that he wanted to go to church with his mother. A lady greeted them in the foyer, wrinkling her nose. "This is your son? I didn't know you even had a son ..." Sherri drew her bleary-eyed boy into a strong hug and sprang to his defense: "Yes, he's ours, and we love him so very much."

And they began to understand why some marriages with prodigal kids implode under that huge weight. Steve felt like quitting ministry and heading off to a minimum-wage job in Hawaii: "I wanted to run, not from Sherri or Craig, but from *responsibility*. I didn't want that anymore." Of course there were times of friction between Sherri and Steve, because they would switch roles back and forth, one wanting to be more firm, the other more compassionate. Conflict was the inevitable result. Each needed the other's support, but it was impossible to synchronize. Sometimes both were too burdened to do much more than survive. Unfounded accusations, rooted more in emotion than evidence, were traded back and forth. Old decisions made together were endlessly revisited, and at times each blamed the other for choices that had been made. They tormented themselves with the question, "What if?" It was always a question without an answer.

Love Destabilizes

Loving a prodigal can create seismic instability. Parents are rarely consistent in the ways they approach their prodigals. When your child is in trouble but indignantly protests his innocence, you are forced to quickly decide what and whom to believe. One minute you're raising a cynical eyebrow, perhaps unwittingly joining their false accusers and leaving them stranded. Or perhaps you're exercising real discernment and seeing through the fairy stories. And then the next minute you're opening your mouth wide enough to swallow an obviously outrageous fabrication; the cynic has become the gullible fool. Or maybe it's not just gullibility but self preservation on your part that makes an easy believer out of you. You just don't have the emotional capacity to cope with any more bad news, so you'll accept any old yarn, just for peace of mind. It seems better to tell yourself that all is well and stifle the lingering suspicions you feel, rather than hear more depressing news.

The foundations of your own faith can be shaken. You might navigate periods when you even question the value of being a Christian, in a perverse and desperate defense of your child's poor choices. One way to deal with prodigality is to dismiss the idea of prodigality completely. In moments of despair, especially if you're angry with God anyway, you might tell yourself that all this religious stuff doesn't work and doesn't matter, that your prodigal is no prodigal, that they are just doing life like everybody else—which in a way they are. That conclusion is a deception and won't satisfy, but it's a lie some are willing to buy into for a while.

You might even find yourself strangely envying your prodigal's "freedom," especially if they are in a carefree, high-living phase. After all, you are a human being with a pulse and passions, and sin can look as attractive to you as it can to the guy next door. Even as you think those secret thoughts, you flush with shame. There you are, praying that your prodigal will return to the fold, yet you occasionally feel a day trip to the far country might suit *you* down to the ground. Again, all of this is seductive deception—but these are lies that you might hear whispered convincingly in your ear, so they're worth bringing out into the open.

And then, if you're tempted to camp out for a while in unreality or even be seduced by the same lies that suckered your prodigal, the past can look like a wonderful place to hang out too. You long for what used to be and have to face that the *past*—not outer space—is the final frontier. No one can go there. Steve found himself looking back, wanting the little boy who had been his close buddy. Craig had always adored his dad and loved spending time with him. They golfed, biked, and went to ball games together. All of us should enjoy fond memories, but obsession with them creates a leanness of soul, a lingering, unrequited longing.

But still you want a replay, an opportunity to live once more that carefree twenty minutes of shooting some hoops with your child. You remember their easy, childish giggles, the warmth in their eyes, and you would give almost anything —a fortune, to be sure—to have that moment back again. You didn't realize that time of bouncing around a ball for a while was worth a king's ransom. Perhaps you remember cutting short that playtime because you had some "important" things to do. Ironically, you have absolutely no idea what that important demand was that pulled you away from your child—it was just stuff—but you recall the whoops and the tackles outside in the cold with crystal clarity.

You look back and relive the bedtime routine and the almost throwaway lines: "I love you," and the easy, quick reply, "Love you too." To hear those words again would be the sweetest sound in the world. You open a kitchen drawer, and hid beneath the Yellow Pages, you discover buried treasure: a fading Valentine scrawled with a crayon heart. *I love you, Daddy.* Inside, a poem that would have won no prizes for rhyming, telling you that you were the very best in the world. Now you wonder: Are you loved at all anymore? Do they really hate you like they said in that moment of rage? Is their battle against you, against your God, or do you both stand accused?

Perhaps you feel anger at the way you've been treated. What about all that you have done for them? Ingratitude is a smarting wound to suffer for those who have given for years and then been rejected. In *The Brothers Karamazov*, Dostoyevsky presents a plucky little lady whose ambition is to become a sister of mercy despite her little faith. She believes herself to be "full of strength to overcome all obstacles. No wounds, no festering sores," she says, could frighten her. "I would bind them up, and wash them with my own hands. I would nurse the afflicted. I would be ready to kiss such wounds." But she was less sure about her response if that same patient whose wounds she kissed wasn't grateful for her tender care, or even became abusive or overbearing, "which often happens when people are in great suffering." That would be very difficult to take. "I came with horror to the conclusion that, if anything could dissipate my love to humanity, it would be ingratitude."[3] All of this is compounded by the sense that the one who hurts you has no idea whatsoever of the wounds they inflict—and if they do, perhaps they don't care.

It is said that Sir Isaac Newton, the brilliant scientist, spent weeks working on a thesis about the core of the physical universe, his eyes straining as he scribbled by candlelight, often on the brink of exhaustion. By his side through the weeks sat his beloved dog. One evening, Newton stood up to leave the room for a moment, and the dog tried to follow him, inadvertently bumping into the side of the desk. The candle toppled, set the precious papers ablaze, and in a few moments, weeks of seminal work were reduced to a pile of ashes. Newton was heartbroken when he returned to his study and surveyed the devastation. He rescued what little could be saved, sat down, and placed his head in his hands and wept. And then, gently stroking the dog, he said, "You will never, never know what you have done."

Sometimes returning prodigals are amazed to hear of the hurt their leaving caused.

Led to the Darkest Places

Months or years of suffering ingratitude and rejection might lead you to the darkest questions: Do you love them still, or has the brutal journey pummeled all that love out of you? Have you allowed your heart to grow cold for the sake of self-preservation? Perhaps you make the mistake of trying to measure your love by your emotions and feelings. Rob Parsons writes movingly about the trauma of the parent who has ceased to "feel love":

> I well remember a woman telling me that her thirteen-year-old daughter had driven her to despair. She said, "I hear other parents talk with sadness about the day when their kids leave home and the nest will be empty and yet I cannot wait for my daughter to go. I can't honestly tell you that I do *feel* love for this child."[4]

Of course, love has little to do with feelings. Margie Lewis writes, "Unconditional love is not always an overwhelming, uncontrollable feeling. It is more than just an emotion or a heartfelt warmth. Unconditional love is a conscious choice. And sometimes, when the feelings sag, it may be mostly resolve. It is as much a matter of the mind and will as of the heart."[5]

In your weaker moments, you sometimes wish that you had kept your love under lock and key; and when your heart feels cold toward your prodigal, you might feel nervous about praying for God's divine breath to warm it again, and in doing so, usher in yet more pain.

Steve kept trying to reconnect with Craig, but when he came home for a few days, Steve's offers of a fishing trip, a meal, or a bike ride were always met with a firm no. After a while, Steve stopped offering, too wounded to face yet another installment of rejection.

Conversation became stilted and awkward. When you don't share much time together anymore and your values are in conflict, you end up with the barest bones of conversation: Yes. No. Sure. Whatever.

So what do you talk about? You're uncertain whether to share what's going on in your life, where God and church play such a huge part. Should you give thanks before that one meal you share, or will it be perceived as being preachy and religious, and a backhanded way at giving them a little "dose" of God? And if conversation does flow, it might well end up centering around the same dark issues in your prodigal's life. Their friend who got a DUI. How evil the police are. Their money troubles. That great party they went to.

Sometimes there's nothing to say, and no comment welcome. An excruciating part of this journey is that parents are often required to become silent spectators as those they love make bad and sometimes tragic decisions. As children grow up, their parents get used to making things better: kissing scrapes, meeting teachers, giving rides. They act. And now their hands are tied.

Watching the destruction of a life is a special agony. When Craig showed up with his grinning, bleary-eyed friends, just to say hi before stumbling into another night on the town, Sherri and Steve knew what was ahead in the next few hours. Sometimes they wanted to shake him, to yell, to do anything that would bring him to his senses. But they just bit their lip, shook hands with his pals, and announced that they were pleased to meet them. They would have been pleased to run the whole herd of them out of town, to pry their son from the clutches of this crowd.

Hope began to fade and die for Sherri and Steve. Once they had nursed such high ambitions for Craig, but now they began to expect the worst—better that they be disappointed, or so they thought. The police called to say that they had broken up a rowdy party that Craig had been at—and that he was *not* intoxicated. Steve and Sherri shook their heads and wondered if it was true, for their son was usually stoned.

Love Is More Stern and Splendid Than Kindness

Their praying changed. Gone were the petitions asking that Craig do well in high school, meet the right girl, or find a sense of calling and purpose. Now they just asked God to spare his life. Their fears for his well-being were reasonable; his body was being pounded by his multiple addictions. His lifestyle could have killed him a dozen times.

Steve and Sherri's prayers moved in an unexpected direction. Hesitantly, they began to pray that Craig would feel pain. And their praying taught them the subtle but vital difference between mere kindness and true love.

Love is something far more stern and splendid than kindness. C. S. Lewis writes:

> Kindness ... cares not whether its object becomes good or bad, provided only that it escapes suffering. As Scripture points out, it is bastards who are spoiled: the legitimate sons, who are to carry on the family tradition, are punished. It is for people who we care nothing about that we demand happiness on any terms: with our friends, our lovers, our children, we are exacting and would rather see them suffer much than be happy in contemptible and estranging modes. If God is Love, He is, by definition, something more than mere kindness. And it appears, from all records, that though He has often rebuked and

condemned us, He has never regarded us with contempt. He has paid us the intolerable compliment of loving us, in the deepest, most tragic, most inexorable sense.[6]

So Steve and Sherri paid Craig a compliment of deep, tough love: when he was incarcerated, they desperately wanted to get him out of jail, but they knew that he should probably stay there. Some lessons are only learned when you are locked up in a cell. When parents keep leaping to the rescue, saving their children from the consequences of their poor choices, they haul them out of the classroom of life before any painful lessons are learned. The day of the metha-done/crack overdose, Sherri spoke the most difficult words of her life to Craig. "Dad and I want to help you. But if you ever do this again, don't come home to us—just check your-self into the hospital. We just can't be there to watch you die." Sherri had learned that love is not the same as enabling, that there are times when you have to draw a clear line so as not to allow your child to self-destruct.

Those who have sons or daughters, parents, or siblings who are prodigals are candidates for the greatest pain: the closer the relationship, the more intense the hurt. And single parents surely deserve a book exclusively dedicated to the special challenges they face as they navigate through these issues without the luxury of a partner's shoulder to cry on. Prodigals' friends have quite a fight on their hands too, with many dilemmas to face and questions that seldom have one right answer or a "one-size-fits-all" solution.

Should you go with your friend to the bars and clubs where you know the likelihood is that they'll be abusing alcohol and drugs—is your company compliancy or faithful friend-ship? How much permission do you have in your friendship to be brutally honest about their lifestyle—and will frank conversation be interpreted as unwelcome preaching and drive them further away?

Just sustaining the friendship might well be hard work. The values and priorities that you once shared, that nurtured your friendship in the first place—many of these might not only be gone, but might be a point of major contention. Perhaps you are on the receiving end of angry outbursts about church and God. Are they testing you, too, to see if you will abandon them now that they've decided to walk away?

For those who love prodigals, no experience is the same. But what is common is an overwhelming accumulation of challenges and the one-step-forward-two-steps-back feeling. Just when you thought things were improving, the telephone rings again.

Carrying On with Daily Life

Sherri and Steve were dead tired. The years took their toll, and they felt weary to the bone. Although she was never actually suicidal, Sherri found herself thinking that death would be welcome because then the pain would end. And the day came when she asked Steve to remind her just why they had chosen to have children in the first place. The agony was eclipsing the joy.

What did they do? They did what most parents of prodigals do daily: they carried on with life.

As Christian leaders, they spent their days listening to other people's problems, commiserating with and praying for them, and yet mainly staying silent about the continual ache in their hearts. Sometimes, for hours, they would forget their situation; then it would return, wrapping itself around them like a shroud. At church they kept singing songs about God being faithful and answering prayer. And then the service would end and they would return to a house that had once been Craig's home. Not much evidence of answered prayer there.

Obviously they had to keep parenting their other children. Prodigals can suck all the love out of us, consuming our energy, and we neglect their siblings. One day Sherri was hugging her youngest daughter. When she released her, her daughter protested, snuggling in closer and saying, "Mom, don't let me go just yet."

Resentment can coil itself around the hearts of siblings who are appalled at the damage their brother or sister is wreaking on the family. What family get-togethers there are can therefore be spoiled by crackling tension. No wonder that those who parent prodigals wonder if they really do want them to come to their senses. They pray fervently for a prodigal to have a homecoming back to God—and then guiltily confess that they aren't always so sure they really want them to come home to *their* house, if that is what is involved.

That would mean new pain, disruption; you got on with your life, reorganized your social schedule, and turned that bedroom into an office. You discovered that being an empty nester has some benefits as well as heartaches.

And some parents have confessed those terrible moments when a tragedy would have almost have been welcome; at least it would bring an end to all the uncertainty. One parent is bold enough to say what seems unspeakable:

> I know there is no greater force than love, but we have loved our son until it has broken us. We have bailed him out of police cells and had drug dealers call at our home and threaten us. He has stolen from us, abused us, and brought us close to the edge of insanity. Sometimes we

feel so guilty because we feel it would have been better if he had died. At least then he would be safe. But still we love. We cannot help loving. Only God can help us to love like that.[7]

For Sherri and Steve, the years went by, grinding away in a harsh academy with no graduation day in sight. But sometimes we learn the greatest lessons in the school of hard knocks.

Bless You, Prison

"God is taking you on this difficult road in order to teach you something." The notion, without careful explanation, is dark and dangerous, as if God torches school buses, hands out heart attacks, and scatters cancers where he will, simply so that his hapless and helpless students of life will learn a thing or two. Sherri and Steve knew that God was not the *architect* of their pain, but that he could be the *redeemer* of it. C. S. Lewis speaks of pain as the "megaphone of God," a term that is rich but perhaps too easily misunderstood, as if God is in the habit of grabbing our attention by mugging us with pain. I don't believe that this is his methodology, but it is clear from Scripture and experience that some fruits can only grow in soil that has been soaked in tears. We spoke of the biblical concept of tribulation earlier, and that unwelcome vineyard of pain is often the place where the best grapes grow.

Frankly, I wish it were not so. Here are a couple of my least favorite Bible verses, truths that I firmly refuse to attach to my refrigerator door: From Romans, "We also rejoice in our sufferings, because we know that suffering produces perseverance; perseverance, character; and character, hope."[8] And from 1 Peter, "But rejoice that you participate in the sufferings of Christ, so that you may be overjoyed when his glory is revealed."[9]

But my dislike of these verses does not make them any less true. Alexander Solzhenitsyn, the Russian dissident who spent years penned in a Siberian Gulag, speaks powerfully of the unique education that pain brings. Looking back, he describes a gratitude for the awful years in that place: "I nourished my soul there, and I say without hesitation: Bless you, prison, for having been in my life."[10]

And so the long night for Steve and Sherri wasn't all bad news; there was soul nourishment for them along the way. In their uphill journey, they saw moments of strange beauty. They became thankful for incidents that were far from incidental, but might otherwise have gone unnoticed and uncelebrated. One night, Craig, high again, came home and asked his mother if she would dye his hair blond. She did, and they ended the evening watching a movie, curled up together on the couch just like in former days. The next morning, she awoke to find him gone. He had left a note saying how thankful he was that she was his mom. She laughed and cried all at once and treasures that note to this day.

Ironically, they learned some lessons about integrity from their son. Prodigals are often more honest about sin; most don't play hypocritical games, and they refuse to pretend they're something they're not. They would rather stay in the far country than try to live in the father's house *and* play on the pig farm.

And they also learned a little about grace from him too. Once, when he went to church with them, a lady squared off at Craig and accused him of being the major influence that had turned her daughter into a partier. When things go wrong, we all want someone to blame, and now Craig was in the firing line. He listened quietly to her raging, apologized, and walked away. And then he whispered to Sherri, "That girl of hers was a party animal way before she ever met me." Sherri was incredulous—why had he stood there and swallowed all that venom? She asked Craig why he didn't defend himself. His answer shocked her more. "What does it matter?"

Through it all, Steve and Sherri's faith reached a new level of maturity. They realized that trust only works in the dark, and that the strongest people are not those who are certain, but those who do faith in the fogbank.

And they mingled hope with a carefully thought-through decision. They knew that God was able to do the impossible in Craig's life. But they were not going to balance their love for him on that hope. And so they made up their minds: they were going to love their son whatever path he chose. They were going to love without any agenda. Whatever else he decided to be, he remained their son.

Sherri and Steve developed a softer, gentler, and perhaps most important of all, a *slower* faith. They were slower to speak, slower to judge, and slower to offer quick, easy answers to complex problems.

By nature, they'd never been blustering, religious bigots, but they learned empathy and became softer and more sympathetic when others fell or had loved ones who did. But they did become a little less tolerant when their "good" Christian friends made faces or joked about people in the church who sported tattoos or multiple piercings. The arrogance of those critics seemed obscene to them. Some of the crude tattoos were undeniably ugly, but that was a matter of taste. Besides, what was more unattractive: a botched eagle in india ink on skin, or a smug, self-righteous heart that consigned another human being to the dumpster because of their appearance?

As they listened to the pious sniggering, they wondered how many people we collide with rather than meet, because we are too quick to judge them by their outward appearance. In the 2005 movie *Crash*, a variety of characters from the Los Angeles populace meet in one fateful day. The key issue in the movie is racial prejudice, but at its heart is the human tendency to prejudge others because something on the surface of their lives causes us to decide that we don't want to look any closer—in short, prejudice. Steve and Sherri wondered how some of their Christian friends must have listened to so many sermons about Jesus reaching out to those marginalized in society and sitting with lepers, prostitutes, and tax collectors. He invested the bulk of his time with people no one wanted anything to do with; ignoring people's prejudices, he just accepted people as people. How could it be possible to worship a Jesus like this and still be so quick to write off those who don't look or sound like us?

Sherri and Steve were pained not only by their prodigal, but increasingly by the attitudes of those who considered themselves very much "at home."

They learned to be part of the fellowship of the helpless —those who have learned that there are times when all you can do is wait and watch helplessly, and that the Christian doesn't have to fear powerlessness. On the contrary, there is something liberating about kneeling helplessly before an all-powerful God.

They gained a new sensitivity toward each other and learned to look out for telltale signs that the other was struggling. Sometimes just a smile or a wink shared between them during church was enough to sustain them through another difficult moment. And during long conversations, sometimes whispered in the small hours, they found a vocabulary to express not only what was happening, but what they *felt* about what was happening.

In time, and in retrospect, it was a prison experience that they too would come to bless. But it was a prison still, with no hint of parole to come.

chapter three

Who Are the Prodigals?

*I suffer whenever I see that common sight of a parent
or senior imposing his opinion and way of thinking
and being on a young soul to which he is totally unfit.
Cannot we let people be themselves and enjoy life in their own way?
You are trying to make another you. One's enough.*

EMERSON

Sherri and Steve were just one couple among millions who
wept for their prodigal. I think of another couple who became so desperately concerned for their son, that they planned
to kidnap him. Wearied and worried by news of the scandal-
ous antics of their son, his parents called an emergency family conference; together they agreed to take matters into their
own hands. Why wait until it was too late, until their son and
their brother was just a stiffened corpse to bring home and
bury? Rumor had it that he was the talk of the town, so eccentric was his behavior, most likely the result of a complete
nervous breakdown. That was the final straw. Unable to decide anything sensible for himself, he needed protection from
his own madness. He may hate them for it, but it was for his
own good. Wherever he was, they would hunt him down and

snatch him from the grasp of his so-called friends. Like it or not, their prodigal was coming home.

From the beginning, his parents knew that their oldest boy would bring them great joy and terrible pain. The first sign of difficulties ahead came when, years earlier, he had suddenly disappeared without warning and they endured a nerve-wracking couple of days wondering if he was alive or dead. Finally he was found safe, but his explanation for his absence was odd and unnerving, to say the least. Things were calm for quite a while, and then came the storm. He started hanging out with the wrong crowd and became Mr. Popular in his somewhat-dubious social set. A number of local ministers heard about his lifestyle and loudly announced their disgust. Shame on him and his family, they said. His standards, or lack of them, were appalling. He showed no respect, they said. They even suggested that he had toyed with satanism and that his weirdness was Devil-driven. The crisis finally came to a head when the news filtered back that their "prodigal" was spending so much time hanging out in the rough part of town that he wasn't even taking time to eat or take basic care of himself. In desperation, the family went looking for him. He was easy to find, the colorful center of attention yet again.

But their mission was a failure. Surrounded by his pals, he refused even to talk to his family and carried on as if they weren't there. They returned home bitterly disappointed, frantically anxious about their prodigal. If he carried on like this, he was going to get himself killed. And within a couple of years, their fears were realized; he died in writhing agony, his mother at his side, helpless to rescue him.

"Mom" was called Mary. Her "prodigal" son was Jesus, who went walking in the temple courts,[1] who enjoyed the company of the worst kinds of people,[2] and who gave the local ministers (the scribes and Pharisees) apoplexy when he refused to jump through their man-made religious hoops or play their little games.[3] Outraged, they accused him of being motivated and inhabited by demons.[4] And that attempted rescue bid/kidnapping by his family came when Jesus was rumored to be so busy in his teaching, healing, and deliverance ministry that he didn't even have time to eat.[5] His family thought he was crazy and sought to take him home by force.

What looked like prodigality was anything but. Yet through some people's eyes, especially those closest to him, he *looked* like a prodigal because he refused to stay within the time-honored boundaries of their traditions. He shrugged off their expectations and demands, and created a scandal when he rejected their lifeless religiosity. They gasped and muttered and feared that he was dancing to the Devil's tune, when he was actually walking in perfect step with his Father.[6] The religious police of the day, perhaps like us, figured a woman or man to be guilty by association; judging the motley crew that he called his friends, he was, to them, a prodigal.

And the sight of Jesus ultimately skewered onto a cross looked like the sad finale to a bad life; the cross was the ultimate sign of disgrace, a far-country symbol. But there, when he was apparently down and out, the greatest work of universal history was done, and up from the grave he arose.

That's why we need to pause and think before we slap a huge label marked "prodigal" on someone. Let's remind ourselves that the parable of the prodigal son was told in the first place as a response to labeling. The religious experts of the day habitually scrawled the word "sinner" over certain people they didn't approve of—and then wrote them off as being beyond the love of God. Jesus objected to their hasty and unjust categorizing and so told the beautiful story. Ironically, we can misuse that very same parable and make a new labeling machine of our own.

Jesus never used the word "prodigal" at all—it's not in the biblical text but appears in the paragraph break in most Bibles because "The Parable of the Prodigal Son" is the name by which this story has become commonly known. But never once in his telling of the story does Jesus tag the wayward boy in this way. At home, in the far country, and as guest of honor at the homecoming party, he is always faithfully described the same way: as the younger son. We are using the term "prodigals" in the title and content of this book, but we do so for purposes of shorthand only, as an inadequate coverall to describe someone who is evidently or apparently away from God. But it must remain shorthand and never develop into a label, for such labeling could actually provoke people to walk from God.

And then the parable that Jesus told is cut and dried, the characters clearly defined: father, elder brother, and younger son. The story is told not as a complex commentary on parenting or relationships, but as a fairly simple (yet colorful) saga about lostness, love, and religion. The young son walks because he wants to sin, the elder brother boycotts the party as a protest against grace, and the father loves flamboyantly, because that's what God the Father does. It's all very straightforward. But the parable doesn't work as a rigid template to definitively explain why people walk or drift away from church and perhaps God. Prodigality is more complex than that.

Some people might well be running, but we will see they are out there on those lonely hills looking *for* God, not trying to evade him. Perhaps it's startling, and maybe it's a relief, but consider this: some of our so-called prodigals are not prodigals at all. Before we pray for them to come home, let's make sure they really have left. Are they prodigals or restless exiles, some of them so desperate for truth that they have fled the comfortable warmth of the pew to try to find it? When it comes to prodigality, we have a sad tendency to confuse *the father and his house* with the *institution called the church*. And when we do that, we wrongly assume that those who are lost from church have also abandoned God. Some so-called prodigals don't warrant that name.

And then there are those who genuinely *are* fugitives from Jesus, but they don't flee for one reason alone, which is why excessive parallels with the parable are unhelpful. Some of them may end up with the pigs, but a number of factors will have contributed to the journey that got them there. If we are to see a homecoming, we must think carefully about the factors that caused them to walk away in the first place.

In developing our discussion along these lines, I'm aware that we can be yet again tempted to pigeonhole people—is our prodigal an exile on the hunt for truth, or a rebel on the lookout for the wild life? Again, let's avoid hasty categorization. Many are a mixture of both. But perhaps to make this distinction will be helpful for now.

Excursion into Sin, or Expedition in Search of Reality?

Some of those whom we think are rushing to the far country are actually genuinely looking for the city of God. They drop out of church not because they don't care, but because they care too much. They won't play along with a Sunday morning religious charade that is utterly disconnected with Monday morning reality.

Far from being fugitives from God, they are fleeing mindless, heartless piety that professes to stretch up to heaven but remains indifferent to the practical and spiritual needs of a hurting world. They are appalled by the sight of hands pressed together in prayer or lifted high in worship, but which then become clenched fists, rigidly closed to the starving. They are frustrated by the ridiculous notion that the cross and the flag of their country belong side by side, by the flimsy nationalism that insists that God in heaven always supports whatever their nation or government chooses to do. And they are right to be angry.

For these restless wanderers, Christianity has not proved to be significant enough to invest in. They are looking for something to live and die for, not to fill an hour-long gap on a rainy Sunday morning. They don't want to pray for thirty minutes; if prayer is worth the effort, they'd like to pray through the night. They are unwilling to be bored today for fire insurance tomorrow.

Some of them have been converted, but not enchanted. They've worked their way through *The Four Spiritual Laws* with the passion of someone reading a real estate contract. They made a deal to cover life after death, but it was unsustainable for their lives before death. The commentator Walter Brueggemann calls all of us to rediscover the breathtaking, big story of God:

> The story that tells you who you are is not the story of your parents, ancestors, ethnic group or social class. It is, instead, the story of the Bible—the promise to Abraham, deliverance from slavery to Egypt and sin, and the gift of land to landless Israelites and life to dead sinners. This story of promise, deliverance and gift is your family his-

tory, the story that defines you. The call of evangelism is to switch stories and therefore to change lives.[7]

But some of our prodigals have never had their imagination aroused by that huge epic story. They have never been shaken or stirred, broken or enthralled; just informed that church is where good, God-fearing people hang out on Sundays. They have prayed a sinner's prayer, but never switched stories. They bumped into mild piety, but never sensed the heady winds of destiny blowing through their hair. Faith for them has been something of a foundation, but never something earth shaking.

So some of them—not all—genuinely desire something better. And even though their search may take them down some dark, blind alleyways, their crisis is often more philosophical than moral. It is not that they want to sin spectacularly; rather they desire to be more serious saints, as perhaps for the first time in their lives they wrestle with huge, awkward questions.

Some of us who "stay at home" have been troubled by those issues, but we made an uneasy truce with such disturbing thoughts. Perhaps we didn't want to rock the religious boat, or we felt intimidated by issues that appeared too big to tackle, so we filed our concerns away under "pending" and just carried on singing the hymns. But for some so-called prodigals, what niggled them now haunts them.

They have theological worries and want to believe in the three-in-one mystery that is the Trinity, but would just like to air their questions about the complexities of that truth in a safe place where they wouldn't be dubbed as heretics just for asking. On the same Sunday, they hear about God's love and compassion, along with news of the crackling bonfires of hell, and they fret about how it all fits together.

They are troubled by the preacher who never smiles about sex (unless he cracks one of his anti-gay jokes) and are depressed by the strange-haired evangelist on Christian TV who warns—weekly, without fail—that his ministry is going bankrupt ("Pray and write that check right now, in Jesus' name!"). He also says a tsunami is a judgment wake-up call from a God who is mad with pagans, but who apparently doesn't make waves—literally—for Wall Street devotees of the dollar. And prodigals fret about sermons on creation that fight a bloody battle against the sworn enemy that is evolution, but never have environmentalism as their third point. They shove their heads between their hands when they are in a service where people are being prayed over and fall to the ground—as a result of a pushing, shoving evangelist. They really wanted to believe that the line of prone folks at the front are there due to the activity of God—it's just that they heard the slap of a hand on the forehead and saw that hard shove with their own eyes. They are troubled when healings are prematurely announced and celebrated, when the incredible answer to prayer that caused congregational euphoria turns out to be only a tragically temporary remission. Perhaps it's followed by a funeral and mildly embarrassed silence, or clichés such as, "The Lord decided to take him home." Won't someone be brave enough to call the death of that young mother of three what it really is—a tragedy?

And something nags at them when it is announced that a good thing happened, and therefore God is good. Does that mean that when bad things take place, God is conversely bad? They wonder quietly why God always gets the credit and the Devil gets the blame. And they are rightly nervous about trivial religion. God may actually be interested in the provision of parking spaces for his people in a world where people stop breathing every second due to lack of food. But if he is, they ask, then why?

In many churches, questions such as these are discouraged, intellectual dialogue is frowned upon, and to confess doubt is tantamount to admitting suffering an outbreak of herpes. And so some agonize alone over these and other difficult issues.

Churches with excessively strong leaders tend to get nervous when someone asks "awkward" questions. Some of them even tag people with inquiring minds as "divisive"—but often they are just genuine seekers, hunting for answers to some perfectly reasonable questions.

> When people, especially Christians, do ask questions, we raise our eyebrows in alarm. The reason for this is that often we don't know the answers, and we feel that if we don't give answers, we shall lose our ability to control what happens to us and to others. This is especially true of ministers and Christian leaders, but it's also true of Christians generally. Questions are a threat to faith and order. This is one of the reasons the Pharisees and other leaders of Jesus' day found the carpenter of Galilee such a pain; he was always questioning why they did the things they did.[8]

Too often, believers are fed superficial and unsustainable answers that fall apart with even momentary examination. One young man (now anything but a prodigal) expressed:

> I remember as a boy getting ready for the church service every Sunday morning. My mother would make me dress up for the occasion. I had to wear a suit, which would have been fine had it not been made out of the most hideous tartan fabric. If I felt ridiculous walking to church

I'm sure it was nothing compared to how ridiculous I looked.

One Sunday I plucked up the courage to ask my Mum why I had to wear that stupid tartan suit. She replied, "If you were going to see the queen you'd dress up, wouldn't you?" It was hard to disagree. "Well," she continued, "you're going to see the King of Kings!" The problem was that even as a child I could see the flaw in my mother's argument. If God was who he claimed to be then he was everywhere, not just shut up in a stuffy, old church building. Therefore, he didn't just see me in my suit; he saw me all the time—whether I was dressed in smart clothes, scruffy clothes or no clothes at all. I was forced to conclude that it wasn't God I was wearing the suit for at all; it was all of the other people at the service. But those clothes gave a completely false impression of who I really was. So it was that, even at that young age, going to church had become synonymous with pretending to be something that I was not.[9]

Not only was this young man's reasonable question answered with a total falsehood, but he was forced to live under the shadow of that error. It's a wonder he didn't walk away back then, instead of becoming the fine Christian leader he is today. He obediently wore the suit, but thankfully, refused to put up with a hand-me-down faith.

But others struggle and think, and exhausted by their Sunday morning appointment with angst, they walk away from the institution. They know that they don't quite fit with their awkward questions. We should not rush to conclude that they are spiritually bankrupt. Perhaps they are more desperate for authenticity and truth, and therefore are more profoundly spiritual than many of us "respectable"

Christians. Some of them are actually brave pioneers, even though the establishment—are *we* the establishment?—will tend to tag them as prodigals. William Wilberforce, the now-celebrated English member of Parliament who tirelessly campaigned for the abolition of slavery in the British Empire, was attacked for his "damnable doctrines" by Admiral Lord Nelson—the heroic figure whose statue stands atop Nelson's Column in central London today. Some Christians wrote off Wilberforce and refused to cooperate with him because they mistook his genius as a political tactician as compromise. Others hated him because he was critical of the safe, nominal Christianity that smothered eighteenth-century Britain. Some of the greatest pioneers of our time were designated as prodigals while they lived; only history looks back and applauds them as the true pioneers that they really were.

Like Bono of the rock band *U2*, many still haven't found what they are looking for. They are entirely right to keep looking. And some of them are running from legalism, a small word that covers a multitude of sins. The Pharisees of Jesus' day had turned faith into a stifling straitjacket. Their God was difficult—actually impossible—to please, and they were like him. There were rules and regulations that sapped the joy out of even the most sparkling moments of life, with legislation even about how to greet a bride on her wedding day. Moments of spontaneous compassion were smothered by their little lists—there was a regulation about how to comfort a widow at a funeral. And even the most ordinary domestic tasks didn't escape their attention: one was not supposed to look into a mirror on the Sabbath, for there was a danger that you might find a stray grey hair and be tempted to pluck it out. In doing so, work would have been done and sin committed.

It's often been said that evangelical Christians are the natural heirs of the Pharisees. We too have our lists of many man-made dos and don'ts. The rules usually vary from church to church, which isn't surprising—their inconsistency testifies to their lack of biblical foundation. And some of the rules are illogical as well as extrabiblical. Some Christians don't go to movies—but they own a VCR and a DVD player, so they watch the same movies, only at a later time. Others have regulations about wearing makeup, jewelry, and head coverings. They've turned their preferences into laws when they absolutely prescribe matters of which version of the Bible should be used, wearing suits on Sundays, and the use of alcohol. One church I know even had a rule that "holy" women should also be hairy women, seeing as they were not allowed to shave their legs. Many of those that we might be tempted to tag as prodigals are actually on the run from this brand of religion with its accompanying madness. May they sprint faster; I wish them Godspeed.

I'm with the Band, Not with the Church

It was an enchanting New Year's Eve. Razor-creased tuxedos and colorful cocktail dresses abounded at a dinner dance. The band was talented, and I was enjoying the sight of graceful couples swishing around the dance floor. And then, during a musical break, the lead singer from the band came over to our table. She recognized friends that we were with and knew that we were all Christian leaders. She was smiling, but tearful. "I can't tell you how much it means to me that you are all here," she said, "enjoying yourselves, actually having fun—and *you*, not only Christians, but leaders too."

She went on to tell us some of her harrowing story. Raised in a church that preached grace but lived law, she learned rather quickly that hell was really easy to get into: all you had to do was break one of the many little legislations that her church had set up as God's law, and you'd be heading for the pit, pronto. She told us about principles of holiness that had nothing to do with genuine biblical standards at all. There were extreme rules about modesty that were always focused on restricting women and had not a hint of logic about them. Women were not allowed to wear jeans in her church, as "jeans were what men wear, and females should look female, and males look male." My jaw fell open. My wife wears jeans almost every day, and never once have I mistaken her for a chap.

Her church espoused a smug exclusivism, where contact with "worldly people" outside of the church family was strongly discouraged. They supported separatist teaching with blatant misuse of Scripture; Paul's encouragement to God's people to be "separate" from the world was twisted from being the call for us to live distinctive lives *in* the world into a warped command that all Christians piously distance themselves *from* the world.[10]

And then she told us how her "godly" parents now wanted nothing more to do with her, flatly announcing that they no longer had a daughter and that she was surely hell-bound. They had denounced her in a bile-filled letter, saying how very proud they were of all their children — except her, and how she had been such a disappointment to one member of their family who had since died. Not only had she been raised with mindless rules, but she had been fed a diet of constant disapproval too. There had been a famine of encouragement in her home.

Some of our prodigals have walked away because, like our singer friend, they've rarely been caught doing something right. Instead, they've been caught doing things very "wrong," seeing as how God apparently cannot tolerate people who sing in dance bands.

And apparently he's not too keen on black people either. The last straw came when she took a homeless black friend to meet her parents, thinking they might extend a welcome to him in Jesus' name. There was no finesse in their refusal: they wanted nothing to do with him, and her father's twisted rhetoric made it clear where he stood. Homeless was bad enough; black was worse.

Racism is appalling, but prejudice peppered with quotations from the Bible is especially nauseating.

Our singer friend felt very lost, not fully at home with what she was doing, a woman torn between two warring worlds. She had to learn all the "classic" songs that the band performed, because radios had been banned from her family home. She said she'd tried to get back into "the church thing," but always felt so condemned and unworthy. She belonged nowhere.

As we raised our glasses and proposed a toast to her, I wondered how many millions have given up on church—and sometimes God—because of nonsensical, illogical, unbiblical teaching spouted from too many pulpits with such authority and ignorance.

Living by Taboos

Here I must be careful, because I'm liable to get a little too angry and forget that most legalistic religion is perpetuated by classically *good* people. While the racism and hatred that I just described is indefensible, the fact remains that those who continue to insist on living by their little taboos (and demand that others join them) genuinely think they are being faithful to God in their crusade. In many cases, they themselves have spent years being threatened with an eternal barbecuing if they don't toe the legalistic line. We fear that if we ask awkward questions, then we are betraying our roots, our upbringing, and, most of all, our God. The awful power of legalism rests in its subtle capacity to convince us that it is the truth, and that God will only be pleased with us if we live by that perceived truth. Surely, on a grander and darker scale, that's the power of fundamentalist terrorism: devout people steer aircraft full of screaming innocents into high-rise buildings, while all the time believing that they do God a favor.

I think of Jesus' eyes ablaze with indignation as he renounced the religious bigots of his day for their pernickety insistence that everyone do religion *their* way rather than God's.[11] I'm stunned by Paul the apostle (never one to mince his words) addressing the Galatian teachers who demanded circumcision from Gentile converts. He suggested that they go the whole way and castrate themselves.[12] He was so incensed as he saw those who were discovering new freedom in Christ being herded and harassed by the religious police of the day.

I think of a lady who attended our church with her teenage daughter. The seventeen-year-old was wearing thong underwear that is designed to show. As they settled into their pew, the mother heard muttering behind her and realized that a couple back there were expressing their disgust, loud and clear, that a young woman should come into "the house of God" dressed in such a sleazy manner. Mom turned around quickly and emptied both barrels. "This is the first time my lovely daughter has been in a church service for a very long time. I'm just delighted she's here, and I'm rather certain God is too. I'd be grateful if you could keep your muttering down." I applaud her; how tragic it would have been if that young girl had heard nothing other than disapproval that day and had been left stranded by an embarrassed mother. It never occurred to the whispering critics that there are more important issues than a piece of elastic stretched across someone's back. But often legalism flourishes where we react without thinking, rather than allowing space and time for common sense to win through.

Combating legalism demands that we do the hard work of thinking faith through for ourselves. Surely Tony Campolo is right when he suggests that legalism is actually the result of laziness:

> It is possible in any church to find people who want to be part of the group, not because they find that the orthodox positions of Christianity are true, but because they do not want to think and work out the meaning of the Bible through honest labor. They find it easier to believe things to be true because some authoritarian person declares them to be true. They accept what they are taught without evaluation or question.[13]

It takes a lot of effort and energy to think faith through for ourselves and to agonize over our ethics and morality. It's a lot less taxing to just accept whatever we're told about how Christians are supposed to live. But unless we are prepared to roll up our sleeves and ask questions about ridiculous laws that make no sense, we will continue to see prodigals created at factory-efficient speed.

Bravery Needed

Perhaps we back away from challenging legalism because we are afraid. If we challenge the legalistic status quo, we risk the condemnation of others, some of whom we might love and respect. Those who challenge legalism usually end up looking like liberals. It takes guts to journey out of legalistic religion, but that exodus may be one of the most authentically Christian, godly treks we ever take.

Sometime after World War 2, during the reconstruction of Europe, the World Council of Churches wanted to see how its money was being spent in some remote parts of the Balkan Peninsula. Accordingly, it despatched John Mackie, who was then president of the Church of Scotland, and two brothers in the cloth of another denomination—a rather severe and pietistic denomination—to take a jeep and travel to some of the villages where the funds were being disbursed. One afternoon, Dr. Mackie and the other two clergymen went to call on the Orthodox priest in a small Greek village. The priest was overjoyed to see them, and was eager to pay his respects. Immediately, he produced a box of Havana cigars, a great treasure in those days, and offered each of his guests a cigar. Dr. Mackie took one; bit the end off, lit it, puffed a few puffs, and said how good it was. The other gentlemen looked horrified and said, "No, thank you, we don't smoke."

Realizing he had somehow offended the two who refused, the priest was anxious to make amends. So he excused himself and reappeared in a few minutes with a flagon of his choicest wine. Dr. Mackie took a glassful, sniffed it like a connoisseur, sipped it and praised its quality. Soon he asked for another glass. His companions, however, drew themselves back even more noticeably than before and said, "No, thank you, we don't drink!" Later, when the three men were in the jeep again, making their way up the rough road out of the village, the two pious clergymen turned on Dr. Mackie with a vengeance. "Dr. Mackie," they insisted, "do you mean to tell us that you are president of the Church of Scotland and an officer of the World Council of Churches and you smoke and drink?"

Dr. Mackie had had all he could take, and his Scottish temper got the better of him. "No, I don't," he said, "but *somebody* had to be a Christian!"[14]

Meanwhile, back at New Year's Eve, I wanted to congratulate the band singer for not being part of that church anymore. I only heard one side of the story, and she desperately needs to be part of a healthy community of faith. But that little church of hers has turned into a cult, and she's better off out of it.

Not as Advertised

Some are prodigals, both from God *and* church, because they are desperately disappointed. In becoming Christians, they responded to an offer and made a commitment, but then found out that all was not as advertised. It's frustrating to commit to a product, only to find out that the convincing arguments that swayed you into buying the thing were misleading, and that it doesn't deliver what was promised.

Consider some of the language that we Christians use when we get together. I fear that we can describe the "product" that is Christianity in a way that is just a little short on truth. I'm not suggesting any sleight-of-hand skullduggery here, but much of the time we talk about being followers of Christ in shorthand vocabulary that can give a false impression. We affirm that prayer is a delightful privilege—and indeed it is—but we fail to mention that it can be rather hard work sustaining what is most often a one-way conversation. We announce that God has spoken to us, and again, he does. But frequently we don't qualify our words, so that others are left believing that we begin our days by tuning into a booming voice in the bathroom. What we usually mean is that we have a sense, a holy hunch, and an internal battle as we ask, "Does that persistent idea keep floating around my head because God is actually speaking, the Devil is distracting, or the pepperoni pizza we ate last night repeating?" But our quick summaries suggest that we are enjoying twenty-four-hour, broadband-clarity communication with the heavenly realms.

Many of us have sat in worship services where an excited leader has quizzed the congregation, "Don't you feel that God is *so* here tonight?" We nod our amens—it seems churlish not to—but the truth is that much of the time we come to worship with absolutely no warm, fuzzy feelings whatsoever. Only this morning I sat through a church service, struggling with irrational guilt because I didn't *feel* more. But isn't worship more about faithful obedience than an emotional high? Surely sung worship, for example, is not something I always feel like doing, but is something I do to align my head and heart with the truths that are forever true, whatever my emotional state. But I look around, and everyone else seems so naturally inclined towards singing that song through for the thirteenth time that I fear that it is only me—and perhaps odd chaps such as Paul the apostle—who experience such internal mayhem.

So I find this law at work: When I want to do good, evil is right there with me. For in my inner being I delight in God's law; but I see another law at work in the members of my body, waging war against the law of my mind and making me a prisoner of the law of sin at work within my members. What a wretched man I am! Who will rescue me from this body of death?[15]

Let's be careful how we describe this life of faith, lest we make prodigals out of disappointed, disillusioned people who are not really rejecting faith, but a facsimile of faith created by our accumulated careless words. Be determined to tell it the way it is—the good news is good enough and requires no false gloss.

Pummeled into Prodigality

It was one of the ugliest sights of my life. As I looked down at the broken, blood-spattered body before me, my stomach heaved at the violence of the moment. The man had literally been punched through the windows of a bar. As we had walked past the place, suddenly the window frame exploded and he came flying through, glass and blood spraying everywhere. He landed on his head with a sickening thud. No one came running out of the bar to continue the beating or to check for a pulse. Within minutes, he was in the emergency room, so drunk he didn't know his name, and confused by the strangers—us—at his bedside.

Some so-called prodigals didn't leave by the door. Figuratively speaking, they were punched through the windows by devastating things done by Bible-clutching despots. I think of one friend who has a grandfather who is an incredible personal evangelist; he loves to make everyone his friend, is thrilled to talk about his wonderful Jesus, and can scarcely get out of a café without pressing prayer on the guy at the next table. Grandpa is a faithful attendee at the weekly prayer meeting and is a walking concordance, so avid a student of Scripture is he.

Grandpa is also a serial rapist, who stole the innocence of his own granddaughters when babysitting them. Recently confronted about his monstrous behavior, he defended himself by saying that his "granddaughter was such a pretty little thing, who was asking for the attention," and besides, "It's all under the blood, you know. Jesus has forgiven me, so what's the point in going over history that he's taken care of?" Little wonder one of those "pretty little things," all grown up now, with emotional bruises that refuse to heal, has experienced the total breakdown of her marriage and now has little time for church.

It makes uncomfortable reading, but allow me to press the point home, lest we are tempted to think that these poundings are isolated, rare instances. Here, another friend tells her story:

> I was in my teens when I got anorexia nervosa and went crazy. I was from a typical strict middle-upper class family, and I was intelligent and pressured to do well. My father was also a church minister who sexually abused me from a very young age. My sanity was ultimately destroyed when I finally discovered that I could never be good enough or do well enough for him. So I started to starve myself. It was the only thing in my life I could find to control—what to eat. I couldn't comply with the perfection that was required of me any longer. So I didn't eat. I hated my body so much that it felt so good to be punishing it and starving it.

Then the depression kicked in, and the anxiety, and then my anorexia turned into bulimia. I would binge and vomit, binge and vomit, binge and vomit. If normal food was not there, then I would eat anything—frozen food still frozen or food from a bin. I went to see a doctor as I hated the bulimia; starving was fine ... but I didn't want to binge. And so I was started on antidepressants and tranquillizers and put under a psychiatrist. I started to spiral deeper and deeper. And then I discovered cutting.

By this time I was abusing alcohol and soft drugs. But cutting was the answer to all my desires. All I had to do was take blades out of razors, lock myself in a room, and cut. I would cut over old cuts if I was running out of room, and soon I was criss-crossed all over. It was great! It didn't hurt much when I did it—the physical pain came later. But I was finally able to give myself what I deserved. I could punish myself really well. I could show the pain that was killing me inside—finally it was visible. My self-hatred grew and grew; or rather the reality of how I saw myself was being expressed more and more. I could not wash or care for myself. I wore all black all the time and attempted suicide several times. I was admitted to a psychiatric hospital several times. My antidepressants and tranquillizers were doubled and then tripled. I gave up vomiting and simply binged as I didn't even care about being thin anymore. I just wanted to be dead.

To compound the tragedy, Susan's father, still a minister, denies his guilt to this day. Those who punch people out of the family of God should tremble. Jesus has strong words for those who cause his little ones to stumble, as he insists that a good fate for them would be drowning in the ocean with a millstone wrapped around the neck.[16] Terrifying language indeed, designed to make us think before we make a fist and throw a punch.

Lost Lambs or Stubborn Rams?

Some prodigals are helpless lambs, their faith easily slaughtered because they were never properly equipped for the battlefield of life. Raised in Christian ghettos, they suddenly find themselves in the real world, and they are bewildered—or enamored. Visit any college campus in America and you'll find plenty of hard-drinking, fast-living Christian kids who never realized before that sin could be such fun. The herd beckons, and the herd is hard to resist. At first they amble into step with the crowd; after a while, they are sprinting in unison with them, accelerating into madness.

Some are intellectually overwhelmed. They have not given faith much thought at all and so are swept away, hit by an avalanche of ideas. Their beliefs were based on what the minister back home served up on Sunday mornings. Mom and Dad just believed whatever the preacher said, apparently without question. But now, their peers and the media conspire to shout down those old notions. Now, the pastor and his simplistic sermons seem to be a fading voice from another world, inadequate for the tough questions of the academy that is life. Donald Miller, who grew up in a pastor's home, said he didn't go through a time of serious rebellion, but he noted that non-rebellion also has its negative side. "If there's a danger in having a father you highly respect and nearly worship," he said, "it's that you may accept his views without checking their validity for yourself."[17] And sometimes, when education, peers, or that college lecturer demand that you do some checking, faith collapses like a deck of cards.

Swill Can Look Swell

Not all who walk do so for reasons that have any idealism or nobility. Some who walk do so not because of disappointment, but because they couldn't care less. There are those who will try to justify their actions by insisting that they were driven into the far country by a deficient church, but some protest too much—they just wanted sin more than sainthood. Apathetic rather than angry at God, they are indifferent and unmoved. It wouldn't matter how socially connected, culturally relevant, and dynamic their church might become—they'd still walk, because those beckoning lights look more inviting than the distant glow of glory.

Without subtlety or pretense, some of them throw themselves headlong into the mire, their sins obvious to all. A friend, ruing the sad truth of her daughter's drift from faith, expressed succinctly, "It's the power of sex. She just wants good sex more than she wants a good life." Her daughter would not accuse that Christian community of driving her into the desert. Her church is relevant, contemporary, relational, and serving its community to the point of exhaustion. Although the church can always do better, it not being perfect, her prodigality is simply not their fault. She just wants the here-and-now rush of love—or even lust—more than the now-but-not-yet hope that her church offers. Let's not rush to make every prodigal exhibit *A* in the case against the church and lay the blame for their exit too quickly at her door.

And some prodigals declare outright war on God and church, so desperate are they to be rid of both. To them, Christianity is too demanding, God is nosily all-knowing, and he threatens to mess up their pursuit of fun. Some of them will become his sworn enemies.

The philosopher Friedrich Nietzsche, famous for his declaration "God is dead," was a prodigal. A theology and philology student at the University of Bonn, he was a minister's son and both his grandfathers were Lutheran ministers. His paternal grandfather, Friedrich August Ludwig Nietzsche, was a distinguished scholar; ironically, one of his books affirmed the "everlasting survival of Christianity." Nietzsche, appalled at the idea of a single, ultimate, judgmental authority who is privy to everyone's hidden, and personally embarrassing, secrets, longed to see the destruction of his grandfather's faith, and proclaimed the death of God.

Friedrich Nietzsche abandoned church and God; his rage at God was clear for all to see. But some drift more quietly. Prodigals don't necessarily abandon their faith in God; their faith just ceases to make much impact upon them anymore. Georges Bernanos declared, "Faith is not a thing which one loses. We merely cease to shape our lives by it." Gradually, subtly, faith becomes irrelevant, and moral erosion begins.

Prodigals in the Pew

Attendance at the pigpen is not required for the prodigal. There are many who stay at home, in church, and look respectable enough not to make a scandal—but whose hearts are still in the far country. What expressions of their faith remain, linger as an old habit—there, but only just. They are prodigals in the pew, woodenly maintaining the church habit while they are bored, indifferent, or even irritated by the weekly religious intrusion.

Consider a modern example. A man has two sons, both of whom are followers of Christ, or so it seems. But the younger one, Jack, has always been a rebel. It was Jack who slipped a live lobster into the baptistery, and Jack, when he was twelve, who spiked the preacher's water jar with vodka and giggled out loud at the slurred sermon. Stephen, in contrast, seemed a model child. He grew up quietly, never one to rock the boat. Whether he was truly saintly or just shy, no one knows, but most assumed that his silence came from someone thoughtful, even spiritual. While Jack bugged his parents with endless awkward questions and seemed to counter every answer with yet another enquiry, Stephen was easy and compliant; he had a beautiful, simple faith, his parents said. But did he?

Jack was an extremist. He didn't just play the drums in church, he beat them to death, prompting complaints from those with hearing aids. He enjoyed swimming in the sea during winter—clothing optional—and would always order the most obscure and exotic food from the menu. Stephen was balanced. He ordered pot roast, gave away just enough money, and insisted on the tax deduction receipt for every penny (good stewardship, he said). He worshiped sincerely, but without a hint of extremism, and could never have been accused of fanaticism.

Jack gave up church when he was twenty. He found it hard to fit in with the Sunday crowd, but he felt right at home in his local bar. Eventually he moved to a big city where he immediately began working with homeless people. It was hard; he was often conned out of the little money he earned and was mugged twice, once at gunpoint. Another time he was arrested for defending a woman who made her home outside a store entrance. A burly security guard was hurling her few meager possessions into a dumpster when Jack intervened—and he ended up spending the day in jail.

He just couldn't stand by and watch helpless people get hurt. Sometimes their pain would make him cry.

The other son, Stephen, never stopped going to church; in fact, he rarely missed a service. He was asked to join the team of deacons, and here he proved to be efficient and dedicated—and completely ineffective. "Yes" was his favorite word, and when he disagreed, he did so in silence. The minister saw him as a rock of unwavering support. But perhaps he just didn't care enough to dissent unless he was affected personally, and even then he kept his frustrations to himself. Stephen actually fumed silently about the worship leader (why don't we sing more hymns?), the youth pastor (why can't he tell those kids not to wear jeans on Sunday morning?), and the single mom whose crying child would occasionally "disturb" the family service. But he smiled a fixed grin and went home to watch the ball game, during which he was occasionally heard shouting.

Which of those two sons is a prodigal? They both are. And they both need to come home.

Is That *Our* Child?

Steve and Sherri had always enjoyed a wide range of music, and so the atmosphere of the rock concert wasn't strange to them. They waited in quiet anticipation for the band that was headlining the event to take the stage. Rumor had it that they were excellent.

Ten minutes into the performance, Sherri found herself overwhelmed by confusion. The young lead singer had a knockout voice, the musicians behind him were musically tight, but between every song the lead singer railed at the audience with a stream of obscenities that made Steve and

Sherri blush. And there was no logic to the outbursts—he just seemed so very angry, he just had to spew some venom. And the young lead singer knew that his parents were in the audience. Craig had just become so accustomed to venting his rage during these concerts, it didn't occur to him that his parents might be disturbed. Sherri looked up at her son ranting again on stage and wondered who he was. What had happened to the boy she had raised; was he still inside Craig somewhere, buried deep by too many dark layers? After the concert was over, Craig, perhaps embarrassed, told them never to attend one of his concerts again.

We're Not Alone

I hope that taking time to reflect a little on the complexity of prodigality has been helpful and prompts you to hesitate rather than rush into simplistic conclusions about those who have drifted from church, wandered from God, or abandoned both.

But whatever the specific circumstances of those whom we think of as prodigals, as we struggle and weep and wait, we share an experience that God feels a billion times daily as he observes his children making a terrible and tragic mess of things.

When you have a loved one who is a prodigal, you suffer a pain like no other. But God really does know how we feel. After all, he's always had trouble with *his* children.

chapter four

God Knows

> The other gods were strong,
> But thou wast weak
> They rode, but thou
> Didst stagger to a throne
> But to our wounds
> Only God's wounds can speak
> And not a god has wounds
> But Thou alone.
>
> **EDWARD SHILLITO, "JESUS OF THE SCARS"**

It's a vicious cocktail, with a scorpion-like sting that can kill you. When you smoke crack cocaine and throw back a large dose of alcohol for a chaser, your heart rate gallops, your liver is bombarded by toxins, and you might fall over. Some people don't ever get up again. That said, you might not be too aware of how badly you've bruised yourself in the fall, because cocaine is also a local anesthetic, which lessens the pain—for a while.

Craig had fallen over, emotionally and physically. He was coming down from the all-too-brief, ten-minute high that crack cocaine promises; now he was free-falling into an emotional valley, and there were additional complications. He couldn't walk; his legs were refusing to obey his brain, which was no surprise, seeing as his brain was broadcasting mush. He was facedown on a fire escape, where he had been all night, and when Steve and Sherri heard the news of his whereabouts, they were relieved.

There had been a flash flood in their city—sixteen people were missing in a disaster that eventually claimed seven lives. The night of the flood, Sherri had taken a call from one of Craig's friends who was worried. Apparently Craig, "invincible" from the crack high, had last been seen wading waist deep into the flood waters. No one had spotted him since, and now his friends were concerned. Sherri had called the hospitals, the jail—anywhere he might possibly be—but with no result. Craig had simply disappeared. Steve and Sherri naturally feared the worst.

The phone rang, bringing the news that Craig had been found safe, but unconscious, on the fire escape. When at last they got him home, he was still out of it.

Steve took Craig's hands and, walking backwards, shuffled and steered him toward the open door of their house. Suddenly, in a second, Steve remembered another moment like this nearly twenty years earlier—a better time. Craig was just under a year old and was determined to take his first steps. His pudgy little legs just wouldn't coordinate. Time after time he would stand up, only to sit right down again on a heavily-padded diaper. And so Steve had taken his little hands and steered him step by step across the room. They made that short journey hundreds of times, until the great day when Craig was finally walking.

It was a huge relief to finally steer him through the house and get him into his bed. He slept soundly, oblivious to all that had happened.

God Knows: Paradise Lost

God has trained a few toddlers to walk, but hopeful days turned quickly to tearful years as his people became oblivious to his help or existence. God sobs through his weeping prophet Hosea: "It was I who taught [them] to walk, taking them by the arms; but they did not realize it was I who healed them."[1] And this has not been a one-off calamity. Throughout history, God has been the cruelly spurned parent. There are some who honestly believe that God the Father is incapable of pain; they call it the "doctrine of impassibility." I respectfully disagree. Mark Stibbe puts it well:

> The Father loves us with a selfless passion. The word passion comes from a Latin word that means suffering. The Father's love for us is a love that costs, that hurts, that suffers.[2]

Nicholas P. Wolterstorff, Professor of Philosophical Theology at Yale Divinity School, says he had to seriously reconsider his theology after the death of his own son. Shattered by grief, Wolterstorff concluded that God could not possibly be unmoved by human tragedy:

> I found that picture of God as blissfully unperturbed by this world's anguish impossible to accept—*existentially* impossible. I could not live with it; I found it grotesque.[3]

God suffers. No one has tasted the bitterness of rejection as he has.

Come with me for a brief wander around Eden. However you interpret the Genesis story, the account paints a rich portrait of exquisite paradise, an utterly splendid place. A walk in that garden of all gardens would leave us wide-eyed with wonder. This was landscaped by the Lord himself. Look over there at those lush green trees, groaning beneath their beautiful burdens of fruit ripe for the picking. And look here: this is the meeting point where four rivers mingle. There's Pishon, which glitters with specks of gold; and Gihon, the Tigris, and the Euphrates.

But Eden was a place of unparalleled beauty not because of location, location, location; it was *parenting* that made it paradise. Here God settled humanity and moved in with them. Listen: you can hear the sound of his footsteps as he strolls around the place in the cool of the day. He was with Adam and Eve as a father is with his children. Determined to be far more to them than the architect who labored over every detail of their design, or the engineering genius who puffed life into their nostrils, he would be the very best parent in history. And what a Father he was.

The kids under his care had it all. Their days were loaded with purpose and play. Surely it was a riotous party time when the beasts and the birds were paraded before Adam and he was invited to give them name tags. Eve arrived, and the pair were to enjoy one another with innocent abandon; together they were to care for their new world.

And they were far more than mere automatons, toys in the hand of the big controller. A stunningly beautiful tree planted right in the heart of the garden symbolized the risky gift of choice that was theirs. Paradise could be lost if they decided to throw it away.

And that's exactly what they did.

They had the perfect environment as their home. The perfect Father lavished them with his loving kindness, and yet still they chose to become the original prodigals and take a walk on the wild side and snatch fruit from *that* tree. Urged on by satanic whispers, they snacked and saw.

It was more than rebellion or mischief. They took that bitter bite because they believed Lucifer's spin. The dark campaign to assassinate God's character succeeded. "Rumor has it," the liar hissed, "he can't be trusted. Rumor has it, that God of yours doesn't mean what he says. He's insecure. Worried you might usurp him with a takeover bid."

The snake never directs the pair to eat; he's too clever to be that obvious. This is a classic seduction, a tantalizing hint followed by a suggestive glimpse of what might be. Prodigals are created as a result of measured strategy. Assaulted by half-truths and a nagging hunger for the forbidden, they eat, believing as they do that perhaps their good God isn't quite so good after all.

And suddenly they don't want to know him as they did. He comes as usual and they run, a pathetic hide-and-seek as they tremble behind the bushes. He knows that they've swallowed the rumors about him along with the fruit. Theirs is a quiet rebellion; no spiteful, vitriolic words tumble from their mouths. But their actions speak louder. They don't want him and the love he offers. All his high hopes and dreams for them dashed, God surely weeps. But it was just the beginning. God's problems with his children have lasted as long as human history, and they continue in this very moment.

Ah, Humanity ...

Some members of the prodigal human race have been loud and abusive in their rejection of God. Stalin, who oversaw the genocide of twenty million of his own people, chose to rage at God with his final breath. His last act on earth was to sit up on his deathbed and shake a clenched fist towards heaven. Many would punch God if they could. God feels their white-hot rage and knows how much they would like to hurt him.

Others wound him with their measured, quiet indifference. God offers outrageous grace, a beautiful invitation, with the request for an RSVP: respond, if you please. But too many just can't be bothered to reply.

In Herman Melville's "Bartleby the Scrivener," Bartleby (the principal character) is a scribe who copies legal documents. The meek and mild Bartleby is liked and appreciated by his employer, but then the boring and previously predictable clerk begins to rebel. Asked to proofread a document, Bartleby refuses and uses a phrase that becomes the theme of the rest of the book: "I'd prefer not to." Soon every request from the employer, no matter how reasonable, is met with the same wooden response: "I'd prefer not to." The employer, who had every reason to fire Bartleby, desperately and yet patiently tries to win him over and coax him with kindness. But eventually Bartleby refuses to do any work at all, and incredibly, makes the office his permanent home and establishes squatter's rights.

Once again his employer is the epitome of longsuffering and kindness, and invites Bartleby to vacate the office building and live in his home; amazing grace that is met by the same monotone, wooden reply: "I'd prefer not to."

Ultimately, the stunningly selfish Bartleby is hauled off to jail, where he goes on a hunger strike. His former employer visits him and pleads with him to take some food. "I'd prefer not to."

As the book ends, the narrator, pondering the polite but unyielding Bartleby, exclaims, "Ah, Bartleby! Ah, humanity."

Perhaps you have been cursed at by an angry prodigal; someone you love has calmly announced that they hate you. Or you've been stonewalled by cold silence. An argument would have been a blessing; even spiteful words would have shown you where they were, providing an opportunity to talk, to whisper encouragement, to yell your own frustration, even defend yourself.

You went the extra mile, perhaps the extra thousand miles, and were gracious to the point that was logically un-reasonable, where you suffered the indignity of being suck-ered, or so it seemed. Did you reach out your hands, offering a warm hug, only to be given the cold shoulder?

God knows; he knows our hurts both intellectually and emotionally. The Hebrew word for "know," *yada*, speaks of a deep emotional experience and bonding between two people, when one is truly able to feel the emotions of the other. This is our God and so he is able to say he *knows* the sufferings of his people;[4] the psalmist is gladdened as he realizes that God knows the troubles of his soul.[5] Again, hear this and allow the truth of it to warm your heart: God knows. He's been there, and he is there still. He's experienced that sink-ing epiphany when you realize that you're being used. You're a commodity, a chef, a cab driver, and you're treated like an ATM: kindly hand over the cash, it's what you are for. Jesus was surrounded by people who were hungry for what he had but showed little sign of wanting him. As they clamored for help and healing, he knew that some wanted to touch his cloak[6] but showed no interest in a conversation, never mind a conversion.

Those whose shoulders have shaken with sobbing, for whom tears come quickly just at the passing thought of their prodigal, can find an empathetic friend in God. Jeremiah announces him as the one whose eyes overflow night and day as he agonizes for his virgin daughter Israel.[7] Have you waited so long for a homecoming? God's daughter gave him grief, not for a moment or a decade, but throughout millennia.

Those Chosen People

> How can I give you up, Ephraim? How can I hand you over, Israel? How can I treat you like Admah? How can I make you like Zeboiim? My heart is changed within me; all my compassion is aroused.[8]

Israel's history reads like a damsel-in-distress story as penned by Stephen King, the master of macabre endings. An imprisoned beauty trapped by a beast within the turrets of a dark castle screams for help. Enter the handsome prince, who scales the flint wall in seconds, fights off a whole herd of ugly heavies, and sweeps the weeping maiden into his arms. Together they rush down the cold stone staircase toward freedom, his sword cutting a bloody swath through yet more thugs dressed up as guards. Finally, they flee the eerie stronghold and gallop off on the prince's trusty steed. Safe at last, the smiling damsel plants a grateful kiss on the prince's cheek—and slides a dagger into his back. As he slumps dying to the ground, his lifeblood a growing pool around him, his eyes are wide with pain, mingled with shock: How could she stab her rescuer?

It's not fiction. Consider those Hebrews, a prodigal nation with a thousand homecomings, punctuated by endless day trips back to the pigpen. When things became unbearable, they'd wail their way back to their God, accept his homecoming gifts, be the guest of honor at the party, and munch on the best beef—only to skip off to that ever-tempting, sinful horizon again. They had been chosen for such an epic destiny. God elected Israel not because he is a selective racist, but because he was looking for a lighthouse people[9] who would not only demonstrate to the nations a life lived under his loving kingship, but reach them with the message of his love too. The temple built at his command was always intended to be a house of prayer *for all the nations*.[10] But they squandered their potential with their breathtaking willfulness.

Take a sixty second look with me at her dubious history, a saga of divine mercy and human stupidity. Promises are made to Father Abraham, who heads out for Canaan, grandson Jacob is born, and then great-grandson arrives, Joseph, that dreamer. A family feud breaks out and Joseph is lobbed in a pit and deserted by everyone — except God,[11] who arranges for the kid to arrive in the land of the Pharaohs as a refugee and to end up as prime minister.

Meanwhile, Canaan is gripped by famine, so Joseph's family heads for Egypt and the hope of a better life. But then, about sixty years after Joseph's funeral, the party ends and the now-numerous Hebrews begin a living nightmare as revolution sweeps through Egypt, and with it, a crude policy of genocide. The Hebrews were hopeless, crushed under the heel of their seemingly omnipotent masters. How they cried.[12] God heard. Moses was born, sent on a boat ride, raised as a prince, and appointed as chief tour guide for the long walk home to Canaan. Those Hebrews never had it so good, but it was never good enough. They crossed the parted Red Sea, helpfully zipped open by God's hand — and a moment of gratitude was followed by a squabble, a crisis of faith, and a threat to murder Moses. And so the story of the prodigal daughter Israel continued, so tediously predictable.

They tired of God and advertised for a replacement king despite Samuel's warning. Suicidal Saul would do. Then came David, weakness and brilliance mingled; Solomon the wise; and Elijah, the prophetic barbecuer who called for fire from heaven and a vote for God from the people. But soon they turn away again. God is grieved; his daughter had become like a sex-obsessed whore. He sends odd prophets to call her home to him. Jeremiah weeps for a lifetime; Amos and a host of other attention-grabbing prophets raged, like Ezekiel, Jeremiah, and the unfortunate Hosea. In a prophetic symbolic action, Isaiah marched around naked and barefoot for three years.

After the close of the Old Testament and a four-hundred-year silence, comes that wildest of Baptists, John. His eyes ablaze with anger, an odd chap with a sweet tooth for honey and a liking for insects, he appears as an explosion in the desert. He grabs the attention of a nation by calling everyone to a baptism of repentance—a real shock tactic in a land where only those who converted to Judaism were baptized, not born-and-bred Jews. Then Jesus comes, God's ultimate Word to a wayward world, comforting those paralyzed by shame, prodding and provoking the religiously smug, infuriating the establishment, and enraging the pious power brokers. Stars track his birth, bleary-eyed shepherds on night shift get the musical show of their lives, wise men trek in with perfume, and kings spit with fury. And just about everybody Jesus ever knew became a prodigal.

And the scene that is Calvary is surely the ultimate gathering of prodigal humanity gone mad. Intoxicated by bloodlust, convinced of their own rightness, they herd around the One who came to rescue them all, and they decorate him with spittle.

So we who weep for prodigals come to him, not just dutifully, and because we should. We come to him not just because we know that the mysterious partnership that is prayer really is effective. We come to him not just because there's no one else to go to with our disappointments, our fears, our broken dreams, and our tormented imaginations.

We come to him because he weeps with those who weep. He's been there before, and he's there now. He can empathize.

German bombers that targeted London during the Second World War finally made their mark on the home of the royal family, Buckingham Palace. The Queen (later to become known as the Queen Mother) remarked that, having gone through the experience, she was now able to look her people in the face. Now her leadership had more credibility because she had shared in the very same sufferings that her people were enduring.

If we weep for a prodigal, we must come to God and look, by faith, at his tears. He is well able to look us in the face—and that look is one of empathy and love.

chapter five

Reasons for Hope

I commit you to the tuition of God.
THE TEMPEST

One of the greatest miracles of the universe is that my television is still in one piece. Insignificant though this seems when stacked up against, say, the feeding of the five thousand or the raising of Lazarus, the health of my television still points to the existence of God, for his grace alone has prevented me more than once from hurling my armchair at the screen.

These fits of rage usually come over me when television preachers proffer their quick-fix slogans, particularly to those who weep for prodigals. I recently watched a silver-tongued preacher masterfully maneuver a crowd of desperate people with a cocktail of guilt, false hope, and the opportunity for them all to seriously damage their Visa cards. "The prodigals are all going to come home!" he declared emphatically, as if the fact that he said it (actually, he yelled it five times) was a sure guarantee that they would. He looked into the camera and told me to ask God how much I should send him. I asked God for permission to send him my leather armchair through the screen, right then. But this is what the crowd longed to hear, of course, and distraught parents hugged each other, their tears of sadness and hopefulness mingled.

I'm sad to say that the hope the preacher gave was false. First off, he used—or more accurately, misused—the best known and most often quoted Scripture about prodigals. You'll recognize it from Proverbs: "Train a child in the way he should go, and when he is old he will not turn from it."[1] The evangelist was excited now. "That's what the Bible says—it's a promise—no ifs, no buts. Either we believe it or not. Who'll claim the promise of Scripture with me here tonight?"

The roar of affirmation was loud—and heartrending.

But the "train up a child" verse is not a surefire, bankable promise that works everywhere, every time. A proverb is a literary device that reveals a general truth. Proverbs are generalizations about life and not promises for us to claim. It is dangerous to lay hold of one or two statements in Proverbs but ignore the total message of the book. For example, Proverbs speaks of barns being filled to overflowing and vats brimming over with new wine,[2] but a recent trip to Ethiopia confirmed the tragic reality: not all believers have full stomachs today, never mind stacked barns.

In many parts of the world, believers who are more passionately devoted to Christ than you or me are dying from famine and poverty. But generally speaking, those who obey God do not ruin their bodies or waste their substance. The book of Proverbs summons us to understand and apply all of God's revealed wisdom for all of life. To hit those parents with a proverb as a promise was a misuse of Scripture. Strike one for the evangelist.

Strike two came when he followed up with that familiar message about faith, which bullies heartbroken people into attempting some mental gymnastics as they try to summon up some more faith. It is "faith in faith," but never fails to convince, seeing as those who love prodigals are suckers for a dose of guilt, as we'll see more of later. "If you don't believe, then no miracle will come for your prodigal." It's the very same technique used to smother people with disabilities who are unable to get out of their wheelchairs on command, or more specifically, on stage. The inference is clear: if the miracle doesn't come, it's *your* fault.

Strike three was inevitable: the financial element of the deal. In a thinly disguised revamp of the medieval Catholic system of indulgences (where the pious parted with cash to get their departed loved ones out of the flames), the preacher implied that the bigger the offering given to his ministry, the greater the likelihood of a miracle in the far country. Unsurprisingly, the offering was huge that night. Three strikes and you're out, I thought, wrestling to pick up my armchair. I was grieved, and not just because I'd witnessed such a misleading, yet masterful piece of fancy footwork.

When false hope is created and then disappointment inevitably follows, some are so devastated they dare not hope again. And when you are longing for a prodigal to come home to God, hope is what gets you out of bed in the morning. What we need is hope, not hype.

So I cannot emphatically tell you that your prodigal *is* coming home. There's no recipe to make that happen, no money-back guaranteed prayer that we can send to the far country. But there are some very good, sound reasons for us keeping the light of hope burning still.

Rob Parsons describes one mother, an elderly lady, who steadfastly refuses to this day to give up hope:

She lives, in a village ... in a large old house. She lives there alone and every night, as darkness falls, she puts a light on in the attic. Her son left home twenty-five years ago, rather like the prodigal in the parable, but she has never given up the hope that one day he will come home. We all know the house well, and although the bulb must occasionally need replacing, none of us have ever seen that house without a light on. It is for her son.[3]

We too need to keep that light burning, and not just because of wishful thinking.

God Goes the Wrong Way

The story is told of a man who very specifically decided to become a full-blown prodigal. His was no gentle slide—he knew what the Lord was asking of him, and in every way possible, he thumbed his nose at God. The man was not quietly rebellious, but loud and angry and petulant. His only prayers were tirades when he spat seething, accusatory words at God. Yet even as he stomped off on the pathway of rebellion, he kept on meeting God there. In fact, he experienced more supernatural phenomena in a few short weeks than most of us see in a lifetime. God used weather patterns to catch his attention, saved the man from certain death by the most bizarre and supernatural rescue, and spoke loudly and clearly in his ears. Even while his heart was still a confused mess, he preached one of the most effective sermons in the history of preaching.

That man was Jonah, the best-known fugitive in the Bible, and God did all of these things I've just described while the prophet was on the run.[4] Even when the petulant prophet finally did agree to accept his mission and go to Nineveh, he did so in a sulk and was outraged when the depraved citizens there decided to repent.

God walked with Jonah even while he walked away, and Jesus strolled with the two on the road to Emmaus[5]—as they walked in precisely the wrong direction. As soon as they realized that Christ was alive, they had to turn around and head back to Jerusalem. I've heard it said that the father in the prodigal story did not go to the far country to help bring his young son home. Helpfully, indeed wonderfully, that is absolutely not the case with God the Father, who doesn't just go to the far country, but lives there as well as everywhere else. Henri Nouwen writes:

> The story of the prodigal son is the story of a God who goes searching for me and who doesn't rest until he has found me. He urges and he pleads. He begs me to stop clinging to the powers of death and to let myself be embraced by arms that will carry me to the place where I will find the life I most desire.[6]

And if we need yet more proof that God works in the lives of those on the run from him, consider the mighty Elijah, who had clay feet, "was just like us,"[7] and became a suicidal prodigal for a while. In a state of sheer terror, Elijah hotfooted it away from the Old Testament "Cruella Deville," Queen Jezebel; he ran for his life and then prayed for death. But while he was still on the run (the first thing that he had to do when he was reconciled once more with God was to go back the way he came) an angel showed up to cook him breakfast.[8] Do not conclude that God walked out of your prodigal's life the moment they walked away from church, and that the only way he will be able to get to them is by you shoehorning them back into a service somewhere. As we'll see, our God is not a localized deity who lives in the church parking lot. He is out there—and he is passionately on a mission. And more than that, God wants to be known. He is not undercover in the far country, playing hide-and-seek with those who have strayed, dropping vague hints of his whereabouts, and making it tough for them to bump into him.

Sometimes the language that celebrates people "finding Jesus" suggests that he was hiding out from them, and that they finally caught him and won the torturous game. Nouwen writes:

> God wants to find me as much as, if not more than, I want to find God.... I am beginning to see how radically the character of my spiritual journey will change when I no longer think of God as hiding out and making it as difficult as possible for me to find him, but instead, is the one who is looking for me while I am doing the hiding.[9]

So much is he the God of the hot pursuit, that one poet famously dubs him "The Hound of Heaven." Francis Thompson studied at Oxford University, England, but got himself ensnared in drug abuse and failed important academic tests more than once, putting his college career at risk. Those who knew Thompson could see the incredible potential and genius he was squandering with his prodigal lifestyle. Thompson ran hard from God, but God ran faster. Thompson's words warrant careful reading and reflection:

> *I fled Him down the nights and down the days*
> *I fled Him down the arches of the years,*
> *I fled Him down the labyrinthine ways*
> *Of my own mind: And in the mist of tears*
> *I hid from Him, and under running laughter*
> *Up vistaed hopes I sped*

Down titanic glooms of chasmed fears
From those strong feet that followed, that followed after
For though I knew His love that followed
Yet I was sore afraid
Lest having Him I have naught else beside.
All that I took from thee I did but take
Not for thy harms
But just that thou might'st seek it in my arms.
All which thy child's mistake fancies are lost
I have stored for thee at home:
"Rise, clasp my hand and come."
Halts by me that footfall:
Is my gloom after all,
Shade of His hand, outstretched caressingly.
Ah, fondest, blindest, weakest,
I am he whom thou seekest!
Thou dravest love from thee, that dravest me.[10]

We can be truly hopeful, because wherever our prodigals are, geographically, emotionally, and spiritually, that Hound has their scent and is on the case. And that Hound won't necessarily need to nudge them into a church building in order to help them come to their senses.

God, Near or Far

The unbiblical description of church buildings as "houses of God" is more than an unfortunate piece of terminology—it leads to corrupt ideas about God and implies that his "house" is where he really lives and engages in his primary activities. I spotted a book written for children about the importance of church. Tragically, there was a cartoon that portrayed a mother and child leaving the church building after a Sunday morning service, with the smiling parent encouraging her child, "Wave good-bye to God until next week, darling." Not only will such terrible error prompt our children to pretend to be angels on Sunday mornings but live like demons on Mondays, but it will limit their and our ability to understand the breadth and scope of God's work, twenty-four/seven. The other extreme to the notion that God is imprisoned in a holy hutch is the idea that God is so far away that he is effectively elsewhere, watching us impassively, as Bette Midler's famous song says, "From a distance." Prayer becomes an exercise akin to lobbing snowballs at the moon (seeing as God is possibly sitting just to the left of Jupiter) and hope for his intervention is virtually nil.

But the good news is that God is dynamically interested and involved in what can be such a mundane world; he refuses to be contained.

Georges Bernanos's classic French novel *The Diary of a Country Priest* ends with the painful death from stomach cancer of a decent young curate, the country priest of the title. Through his difficult life, he appears as a beacon in a dark and dangerous world. The church to which he felt called is beset by corruption and deceit. Bernanos, a devoted Christian and fiercely patriotic Frenchman, presents the good and honest priest as a foil to the excesses of the church of his day. The other priests are self-absorbed and seriously flawed, and Christ's reputation suffers at their hands. As the priest lies dying, we are forced to wonder at the harshness of his struggle. He can no longer keep his diary. Another priest has been called to perform the last rites, but has not yet arrived. We discover the fate and the wisdom of the curate through a letter written by the friend who was with him at the very end:

The priest was still on his way, and finally I was bound to voice my regret that such delay threatened to deprive my comrade of the final consolations of our church. He did not seem to hear me. But a few moments later, he put his hand over mine and his eyes entreated me to draw closer to him. He then uttered these words almost in my ear. And I am quite sure I have recorded them accurately, for his voice, though halting, was strangely distinct. "Does it matter? Grace is everywhere ..." I think he died just then.[11]

The dying priest was right: signs and symbols and touches of grace are all around us, because God wants to interact with us—and with our prodigals.

The Hallelujahing of Creation

God is near, and he wants to get up close and personal. That truth affects our understanding of the world around us. We have evolved an idea that there are "laws" of nature—which seem to imply that there is a coldhearted mechanic or scientist at the heart of the universe. Nature becomes not an ongoing act of creation and sustenance, but a machine of necessity. But God continues his second-by-second play with earth, as a passionate artist.

He is very much here, and not only when he is acknowledged or noticed. That helps us to understand why a piece of gloriously inventive music may be written by someone who doesn't know God; we can admire the masterful use of color and shade on canvas, the work of an artist whose heart is in the far country, and yet who has been kissed, though they don't know it, by the touch of the Creator. Shall we ascribe the source of their creativity to Satan? We must not, because we are living in a God-bathed world.[12]

And wherever in the world your prodigal is, it is in a God-bathed world that they remain. So how will God reach them? The Jesus who was mistaken for a gardener after his resurrection[13] often shows up in the grey, ordinary things of life. Grace can be revealed by great displays of supernatural power, but we are wrong to limit God to the realm of the extraordinary and the remarkable. Of course God has chosen to do these things throughout history, and continues to do so—but grace is to be found all around in the ordinary. Thus God can be found in a painting, in a sunrise, in the innocence of a newborn's eyes, in a rosebud, or in a character in a film or a book; in a song or change of seasons, in the love of friends, and in good food and conversation. People can bump into grace at the coffee shop as well as in the church building.

God can be at work in the most unexpected places. He might choose to grab your prodigal's attention by using a hill and a sunset.

In the Steven Spielberg film *The Color Purple*, Whoopi Goldberg plays a poor, illiterate slave girl. One scene shows her strolling down a dusty lane with a friend. Beside them runs a gnarled fence, and beyond that, a magnificent purple hill, which is crowned by a beautiful blue sky. Goldberg's character softly nudges her friend and smiles gently, saying, "See that? That's God making a pass at us." Who knows what creative, generous expressions of love the Father might be planning for our prodigals? How will he seek to win and woo them today? Perhaps they too might gasp at the sight of a mountain and suddenly stumble into a moment of worship even as they catch their breath.

Calvin Seerfield used the phrase "the hallelujahing of creation" to call us to the recognition that God's creation is a means of revelation and grace. The Bible is emphatic in its assertion that creation is prophetic. It is not itself an object of worship, but it declares the glory of the creator-designer-sustainer God whose genius it so wonderfully conveys.

Creation is ordered to demand a response from human beings; we do not sigh with wonder at the crashing waves or the snowcapped mountains just because we have learned to think that they are attractive. Grace means that creation carries a signature from the Artist, who uses the canvas of land and seascapes, of sunsets and patterns in frost, of color and texture and smell, to help us reconnect with awe. In such a world as this, Tom Bisset reminds us, "There is no escape from the God who is everywhere. He is there and He is ceaselessly calling His own back to the Father's house."[14] And in that world, God has many of his people, and any one of them can be appointed on a special mission to those who are lost in the far country.

God, the Choreographer and Networker

When Craig was walking through a period of especially poor choices, we saw earlier that Steve sometimes wanted to exit "responsibility." One of the deceptions that befalls those who love prodigals is the notion that the prodigal's decision to head for the far country is somehow all about us (it must surely be our poor parenting/friendship/church that has prompted them to walk) and, correspondingly, it is our total responsibility to somehow bring them home. If we pray enough, love enough, and care enough, then we will be the key to a homecoming. In this we are quite wrong; God is perfectly able to choreograph and coordinate the words, kindnesses, friendship, and prayers of others—some of whom we will not know and will never meet—in a concerted effort to express his love to a wandering prodigal. That does not make God's people mere puppets jerked here and there by his choosing, but invites them to the dignity of being junior partners with him in his purposes.

We've probably all experienced those "coincidental" meetings and moments that we call "serendipity." Obviously the ultimate breakthrough of God into our time/space world is the Calvary event, but he continues to interact and engage with his world in serendipitous moments, which may not necessarily be dramatic or miraculous. That "chance" meeting with someone can turn out to be a "divine appointment." Steve and Sherri learned that an old friend of Craig's had shown up at a party and announced that he was now a Christian —a "chance" meeting that was to have a significant impact upon Craig.

Again, God is out there. And let's pause momentarily to remind ourselves of who God is.

God Is, Well, God ...

When we live day in and day out with fears and concerns for a prodigal, one of the most significant effects is that our sense of God's greatness and power can shrink. After all, he seems unwilling—or unable—to do anything to effect a change in the way things are in their lives. Theologian Jim Packer once remarked that "a vision of a pygmy Jesus produces pygmy Christians." Let's remind ourselves that the God to whom we cry is the very same One who thought the universe to be a splendid idea, and so ushered it in with all its unfathomable size, its billions of colors and shades—and all with but a spoken word. This is the God who rolls up seas like an old mat, who breathes life again into the rancid corpse that is Lazarus, who retunes deaf ears and refocuses blind eyes. This is the God who effected the greatest miracle of them all, the fusing together once more of a prodigal humanity to himself by the epic work on the Calvary hill. Death itself couldn't pin him down; the stone is still rolled away.

> One of the traditional readings at Christmas carol services (Isaiah 9) reminds us that we have a God who shatters the yokes that burden people, takes away the heavy bars across their shoulders; breaks the rods of oppressors.... We need a bigger view of God. Is your God One who tears down tyrants from their thrones and sends the rich away empty? Is he One who scatters the proud? Is he the God of the political world as well as your personal world? We have a God who became human, became subject to the laws of physics, and the laws of an occupying force, and the laws of economics, who was pushed around by political whims, who was caught up in the whole human condition—and yet is Lord of it all. If he seems irrelevant to many of our contemporaries, maybe it's because we have confined him to the sacred and kept him out of the real world. We need a bigger view of God.[15]

Coming to God is unlike any other human transaction. The prodigal does not come to him in the same way that he becomes a fan of the Broncos, joins the Republican Party, or decides to join a tennis club. The supernatural, winning, wooing God is at work, and much of what he does, he does without fanfare. Emailed updates from heaven would be helpful, but we must not assume that because we see little measurable progress that no progress is being made.

And he has successfully completed millions of missions thought impossible. Augustine, the great figure of church history, made an early start on sinning. He lived with a mistress when he was just sixteen, fathered an illegitimate child, and then became part of a heretical cult. Many wrote him off as an impossible case. His mother, Monica, asked a bishop to speak with her messed up son and he refused, insisting that only prayer could save him. "Leave him alone for a time.... Only pray to God for him.... Go thy way, and God bless thee, for it is not possible that the son of these tears should perish."[16]

Monica prayed for her son for nineteen years. In his *Confessions*, Augustine tells how "God drew his soul out of the profound darkness." The once-wayward kid became one of the leading bishops in the fourth-century church and a major influence on all Christian history. If God could reach Augustine, there is hope still, for God is still the same.

chapter six

Home Is?

The beginning of love is to let those we love be perfectly themselves, and not to twist them to fit our own image. Otherwise we love only the reflection of ourselves we find in them.

THOMAS MERTON

The title of this book poses at least three questions. We've asked if we are prone to use the word "prodigal" too hastily, because it can describe such a vast variety of conditions and experiences. We've pondered the questioning element of the title, "Will they return home?" and realized that it is a question we must be hopeful about, but not certain, and that false hope does little but cruelly disappoint.

There is a third, challenging question: What do we mean by prodigals "returning home"? If we are to hope and pray for a homecoming, surely we must take time to consider what and where "home" actually is, lest we misdirect our prayers and our hopes, or jump to hasty and inappropriate conclusions. When we want something as desperately as a change of life for prodigals, we can subconsciously develop fixed ideas about what that change will look like, which could be disappointing for us, and far more importantly, devastating for a prodigal trying to find his or her way home to God.

We are in danger of hastily thinking that home is where *we* are, not only physically, but thinking that home is *our* convictions, choice of church, priorities, specific standards of holiness, work ethic, social habits, waking and sleeping patterns, and even politics. Home can symbolize the career hopes that we might quietly nurse, especially for prodigal children, or even some parental aspirations that they might one day be involved in full-time Christian leadership. Home can mean to us that they will wear brown hair instead of bright pink, will have their tattoos removed by laser surgery, and will quickly develop an uncanny affection for gospel country-and-western music. In other words, home is where we are and what we like best. We human beings have an insatiable desire to make people look and act like us; we even attempt to make God conform. Blaise Pascal said that ever since God made humans in his own image, humanity has been trying to return the favor. If we'll try it with God, we'll certainly be tempted to reproduce our image in the lives of those we love.

Once again, we can misuse the beautiful parable of the prodigal. We transpose ourselves into the role of the waiting father, and therefore assume that a homecoming means the prodigal taking the trek back to *our* house, figuratively or literally. But we are not the waiting, perfect father on the farm; that role belongs to God alone, and so true homecoming for the prodigal is a return to *his* warm hearthside, not ours. Obviously, if there has been a breakdown or fracture in our relationship with a prodigal, we pray for a restoration of that too, but let's not confuse or entwine their homecoming to God with their homecoming to us and our opinions and preferences. Ultimately, we remind ourselves that there is no such thing as prodigals that are "ours"; however much we love and long for them, they belong to God, and it's not for us to judge whether they are home or not. But let's not set our prayerful sights on anything less than prodigals having a genuine reconnection with the living God, for that renewal of relationship with him is what "home" really is.

Aiming Low

We live in a culture where nominal Christianity is the norm, and where often all that is needed to prove that you are an "authentic" Christian is fairly frequent Sunday church attendance, the possession of a Bible, and perhaps a fish adorning the back of your vehicle. If a prodigal walks away from God altogether, it's not surprising that we would be thrilled at their return to the very basic *habits* of Christianity—but surely God is looking for *heart* change rather than just the addition of Sunday morning church attendance. While we should be grateful for small victories, a return to the lukewarm, barely-there, nominal fold is not enough to launch a full-blown celebration. Surely such a party is a hollow affair not worth inflating the balloons for. Let's not just pray that the minimums of Christian respectability will emerge in the lives of prodigals; God is not content with a body back in the pew when there's still a heart in the far country.

And let's not back off from praying simply because we hit a wonderful, trouble-free period, a season when perhaps one we love who has been battling with addictions is clean, or when the police don't stop by for their regular little chats anymore. Welcome though that season is, it doesn't constitute a homecoming—a returning prodigal is not just someone who has decided to leave the lifestyle of the far country behind, embracing a more stable existence for a while. A returning prodigal turns not only *from* sin, but *to* God, from survival to full-blown life in Christ. God's heart is not that people are vaguely "good"—but that they are united in intimacy with him. What that relationship will actually look like is for God to judge, and not us.

Home: Our *Brand* of Church?

It was the "Parable of the Prodigal Grandmother," except this particular grandmother had never been an accomplished sinner. There were no heady weekends in Las Vegas for her, no infidelities or brushes with the bottle; she was one of those exceptionally selfless, kind people who apparently didn't need a savior. Of course that's wrong—we're all sinners—but in all the years I knew her, I never once heard one unkind word or saw one thoughtless act. She was my grandmother, she was sweetness personified, and for years she had shown absolutely no interest in God. And then she announced that she was coming to visit us and would be attending the church that I led that Sunday. I never preach sermons with a view to "target" any one person, but obviously I wanted to speak effectively that weekend. This might be the first and last time "Nan" would ever get to hear her grandson preach; more importantly, it would be a great opportunity for her to hear about the love of God in Christ and enjoy the warmth and welcome of our lovely little church family. I prepared carefully and then went to bed Saturday night, anxious about the Sunday morning service to come. All night long I dreamt a bizarre dream, where the biblical sentence, "There is a broad way, and a narrow way"[1] just kept repeating in my mind. I awoke early with a conviction that God had been speaking to me through the dream, scrapped the sermon I'd labored over, and prepared a new talk based around that Scripture.

Grandmother smiled when she walked into church and then proceeded to look relatively bored by everything that took place. I glanced at her as we sang our hymns and prayed our prayers; if she was moved by our worship, she hid it well. When I walked to the pulpit to speak, she looked up and seemed vaguely interested for a minute or two, and then settled back down into apparent disinterest.

And then I read the text that had dominated my dream: "There is a broad way, and a narrow way." I heard a little noise in the congregation and looked over to see my grandmother, tears streaming down her face. It was as if she had suddenly been arrested, the transformation from disinterested spectator to someone who was being profoundly impacted was obvious. She became a Christian at the end of the sermon.

After the service, cup of tea in hand, I asked her what had impacted her so. "All I know is that when you used the phrase about the broad way and the narrow way, in an instant I knew that I needed God. The strange thing is, I still don't really know what those words mean." So much for my informative preaching, but a miracle had happened before our eyes. She was enthusiastic to know what her next steps should be.

Which is where it all went rather wrong. She lived in a tiny village in the south of England, where there was only one local church, a Church of England congregation. This was twenty-five years ago, and I was still prejudiced enough to think that absolutely nothing good could come out of the "C of E," as I dubbed it with disdain. I was also young enough to believe that my particular denomination was the best and really, the only, effective outfit. In my narrow foolishness, I suggested that she attend the nearest church that carried *our* brand name, which was ten miles away. I made no attempt to encourage her to go to the little church down the lane, just a few hundred yards from her cottage.

My prejudiced suggestion was doomed to failure—she had no car, never managed to really connect with the distant church of *my* choice, and didn't become a part of the village congregation that could have been such a lifeline of faith to help her grow in Christ. She died some years later, in faith, but not as someone in a church community. The benefits and blessings of being part of the people of God were not hers—and all because I insisted that her "coming home" meant attending a church of *my* choice. All my prayers, and a supernatural event that brought her to the Lord, didn't prevent me from making the mistake of insisting on a homecoming—my way.

And my narrowness was not just due to arrogance and prejudice. I genuinely believed in my brand of church, was giving my life to church planting for that denomination, and thought that my pointing her to a "home" of my choice was helpful.

Your belief in your church could cause you to do something similar. There are major reasons for your being part of the church family that you call your home. You believe in it, which is why you invest in it. Belief is why you give financially, belief is what makes you prioritize its activities, and belief is what prompts you to invite others to come along to its services. But belief and confidence are but a few footsteps from narrow arrogance. We all live with a lingering suspicion that we and those we hang out with are basically right. Even if we know that our church might not be the "best" in town (however "best" is measured), we consider it to be the best for us. And when the going gets tough in church life (as it invariably does), then we hang in there because we believe that

God wants us to—belief buttressed by a sense of calling. So our choice of church is a matter of conviction and calling, or both, two powerful reasons for a good Baptist to think that home is where Baptists are.

Face it now: it may be that your beloved prodigal might choose to engage with a church that you utterly dislike. Their priorities, liturgy (or lack of it), system of leadership and government, and worship style may be a million miles from where you are. Perhaps "your" returning prodigal might end up in a charismatic church—much to your horror, because you're nervous if anyone scratches their head on Sunday mornings, never mind raises their hands in worship. Or perhaps you're a card-carrying Pentecostal who doesn't feel that real church has truly happened without a hop, a skip, and a prophecy, and now your prodigal is edging towards a church where incense is swung, not the chandeliers, and where people only clap their hands to keep warm when the furnace breaks down. But homecoming is the opening of a heart once more to God, not the opening of our preferred hymnbooks—or the doors of our church building of choice.

Coming Home to Our Approach to Church?

When I became a Christian, good Christian souls went to church twice on a Sunday (morning and evening), great Christians went to Sunday school or adult classes in addition to those two services, and truly spectacular saints showed up for the midweek prayer meeting and Bible study too. This level of attendance was the cultural norm in our lovely little church. Thankfully, there was never any pressure, but there was a sense in which the hearty band of merry young men and women that was our youth group rather expected that level of attendance from each other. And in addition to this, there was Thursday night youth group and Friday night youth club as well. No wonder my parents were a little nervous when I announced that I had converted. They probably thought I'd left home too, so scarcely was I there.

This pattern continued into marriage—literally. Kay and I often look back at our honeymoon, which was a time of much hymn singing and yet more church attendance. Married on Saturday morning, we were bright and early at church on Sunday morning, had tea with the local pastor, and then attended the evening service that night. Sadly, it didn't occur to us that it would be perfectly acceptable for us to have a Sunday clear of religious activities so that we could just spend some time together as newlyweds. That was unthinkable. We were Christians, and Christians go to church at every opportunity, or so we thought.

And then the time came when we became part of a church that didn't have a service on Sunday mornings—we met in the evenings for an incredibly effective gathering, which most weeks saw new people coming to faith. The church was growing at a pace, but it took us quite some time to feel that sleeping in on Sunday morning was not going to warrant a well-directed lightning bolt. Old habits die hard, and sometimes our commitment to doing church the way we do it means that we insist on measuring everybody else by our approach to church life—with disastrous effect.

Rob Parsons writes about how we can unthinkingly insist that the approach of others to "doing" church matches our own—and if it doesn't, then they're "suspect."

A mother and father approached me during an event at which I was speaking in North America. They were in their early sixties and their daughter was seventeen. The father said to me, "We're so worried about our daughter. She's always pushed the boundaries, but now she likes to go dancing on a Friday night."

"Well," I thought to myself, "at least she sounds normal."

The father went on, "Sometimes she likes to go dancing on a Saturday night as well."

"You know," I said, "that's pretty ordinary behaviour for a teenager. There are lots of dangers out there but I've no doubt you've instilled in your daughter what's right and wrong, and in just a few months she'll be an adult."

The mother said, "But she refuses to go to the youth Bible study."

As they spoke I could imagine the scene in their house—this teenager coming downstairs and her parents saying, "You can't go out looking like that," or the rows over whether she can go out again on the Saturday having already been out on the Friday night. My heart went out to this older couple who were doing all they could to keep their girl on the right path, but with the effort practically killing them.

"What's your daughter like around the house?" I asked.

"She's fine," the mother replied. "But as I said, she won't go to the youth Bible study."

"Does she ever go to church with you?" I asked, expecting them to say no, not since she was twelve. They replied, "Every Sunday—she never misses."

"Do you mean to tell me that every Sunday, regardless of how late she comes home the night before, she is in church the next day?" I asked.

"Yes," they answered. "Every Sunday."

"That's incredible!" I said. "When you go home tonight I want you to say to your daughter, 'Darling, we were telling somebody about you tonight and the fact that you are so very faithful every Sunday in coming to church. We felt proud of you.'"

I will never forget what happened next. The mother looked at me and said, "Mr. Parsons, didn't you hear what we said a moment ago? She won't go to the youth Bible study!"

"Forget that for the moment," I said. "Don't always be criticising her for what you think she is doing wrong. Praise her for what she is doing *right*—because if you don't, you're going to have more to worry about than the youth Bible study. It seems to me that at the moment this child is trying to honour God as best she can and she needs every encouragement in that. Don't make a prodigal of your daughter over some mid-week meeting."[2]

Coming Home on the Route of Our Choice?

The prodigal son parable provides a textbook episode of repentance—or does it? At first glance, it seems that the wayward boy is overcome with remorse, throws aside any sense of self-justification, and heads for home, apologies prepared, and willing—desperate even—to join the workforce. Surely we've all dreamed about how a beloved prodigal might return to God. Perhaps a conversation with a work colleague who just happened to be a Christian would prompt hours of heart searching and anguish. Maybe there will be a telephone call out of nowhere, all tears and apologies and promises that life is going to be so different from now on ... or will it be that they will turn up at our door and throw themselves into our arms, a joyful, tearful reunion? Perhaps next Sunday in that little church near where they live, they will slip in for a moment of nostalgia, bump into God, and renew their vows to him. Then they will call from the minister's home to give us the good news ...

Or perhaps they have run out of rent money and have an empty stomach, and need a helping hand again, which was actually why the prodigal in the parable set his compass for home in the first place. Read the story carefully and you'll see that a lack of lunch—and not a moral crisis crippling his conscience—was what set him heading for the homestead. It was only later that the enormity of his insensitivity and sinfulness actually occurred to him.

Instant, "hallelujah I've seen the light" changes are easy to manage—all we have to do is celebrate. But perhaps our prodigals will come home inch by inch, slowly, with lots of baggage and questions and hangers-on as friends, and relapses and rows and sibling conflict for yet more painful years. What really matters is that they come home to God, by whatever route.

Home—the Good Old Days?

Parents of prodigals can make the mistake of believing that when an adult child of theirs turns back to God, they turn back the clock and, in a subtle way, become their children once more. But an adult has graduated from the controls and confessions of a child. When someone we love has spent time in the far country, we can be guilty of thinking that, as part of their repentance to God, they will share every detail of their sad journey with us in the full and frank disclosure of a child. We must face the fact that we may never know those details, and neither do we need to. Some questions will never be answered and never should be, any more than every parent's secrets are known by their children; the dawning of adulthood means that our "access all areas" passes expire.

And a homecoming does not imply the reestablishment of parental authority or control. Lesslie Newbigin said:

> We do not seek to impose our Christian beliefs upon others, but this is not because (as in the liberal view) we recognise that they may be right and we may be wrong. It is because the Christian faith itself, centred in the message of the incarnation, cross and resurrection, forbids the use of any kind of coercive pressure upon others to conform.[3]

Some prodigals avoid any kind of homecoming because it carries with it a stifling, overwhelming threat of conformity, a return to the adolescence that they have left behind. We need to learn how to embrace not the person who was, the one we'd quite like to see re-created, but the person who now is.

Wrestlers use a hug to immobilize and control their opponents. Their arms become a vise of flesh, arm-jaws clamped around the other's body, holding them still, constricting their breathing, and if the "hug" is bearlike enough, ultimately squeezing the life out of them.

Miroslav Volf, a Croatian, knows the bitter aftertaste of ethnic cleansing in former Yugoslavia. He writes about the delightful openness, and potentially suffocating control of a hug:

> An embrace always involves a "double movement" of aperture and closure. I open my arms to create space in myself for the other. The open arms are a sign of discontent at being myself only, and of a desire to include the other. They are an invitation to the other to come in and feel

at home with me, to belong to me. In an embrace I close my arms around the other—not tightly, so as to crush her, or assimilate her forcefully into myself: but gently, so as to tell her that I do not want to be without her in her otherness.[4]

So let's shun the temptation to try to mold them to our shape; we all nurse aspirations for those we love, but our job is to hope quietly, not herd them roughly.

The "R" Word: *Rebellion*

One of the subtle methods that Christian parents and leaders often employ to get things done their way is to describe any behavior patterns that we don't like as *rebellion*. I recently heard about a Christian lady who insists that her son's orange hair must surely be an affront to God—because it is, she says, a sign of her son's rebellion against her. Actually, she is really just insisting that he prefers whatever she prefers in order to show himself to be a good, godly son. But he has passed the age where he needs her permission for his hairstyle. Does it really matter? Leaders sometimes use "the *R* word" when members of their congregation challenge or question them. Suddenly an innocent enquiry is a symptom of a rebellious spirit, and "rebellion is as the sin of witchcraft."[5] These leaders then shun the enquirer or tag them as a troublemaker.

Rebellion is a cover-all word—those who use it always win. I come from a country that has a bloody history of oppression—and much of the bloodletting was done in the name of Christ. The dreadful witch hunts of bygone days are an extreme example.

"Swimming the witch" meant that a mob took a woman who was accused of witchcraft, tied her hands and feet, and threw her into some water to see if she would "swim"—impossible as her limbs were tightly bound. If she succeeded in floating, the crowds concluded that she had been rejected by the water (the mode of baptism) and therefore she was a witch and would be executed. If she drowned, then it was presumed that she had been accepted in the waters of baptism. Even though she was now dead, she was affirmed as posthumously innocent. One writer puts it wryly: "Either way, the hysterical mob got their corpse."[6] When we insist that prodigals who are trying to make their way home to God behave as we command, and we name all attempts at individual expression as rebellious, we may well win the argument —and lose them from the Father's house once more.

> God seems to love diversity—a God who didn't stop
> with a thousand or so insects but conjured up 300,000
> species of beetles and weevils alone, a God who spoke "in
> many and various ways by the prophets,"[7] a God revealed
> in the Galilean who called individuals to himself in very
> distinct ways. [We must not] limit God, setting bound-
> aries on the way he works in His world.[8]

Homecoming Will Demand a New Journey— for All of Us

The homecoming of a prodigal will actually require those who love them the most to go on a new journey to a fresh, uncharted territory in their relationship. We must resist the strong temptation to demand that prodigals return to where they once were, or the greater urge to call them to where we are, even though that place seems quite wonderful to us. Bravery will be needed, because you must be prepared to go with the prodigals to a place that is new to both of you, to an unfamiliar land-scape that neither of you has ever encountered before.

Surely that journey begins afresh today, as we surrender our need to be in control, as we repent of the deception that loving someone allows us to manipulate them, and as we allow God to do what he does best—be God.

The disciples of Jesus often got themselves into trouble when they tried to take over the reins of the operation. If Jesus had followed their suggestions, parents and children would have been sent packing rather than been blessed,[9] a building program would have been launched on the Mount of Transfiguration,[10] sword-swinging Peter would have led an armed rebellion against the Romans,[11] and the feeding of the five thousand would have been cancelled due to tiredness and lack of interest.[12] In fact, Jesus would have never made it to the cross, seeing as some of his friends thought it to be such a terrible idea. Mark, in his gospel, particularly highlights the spectacular ineptitude of these wonderful men who, at times, took on too much responsibility and tried to make things happen that would have been disastrous. Remember, these were good men trying to achieve what they thought was "for the best"—but would have been very much for the worst. The very best that we can do is to release those we love to be all and only what God calls them to be.

Carolyn Ros has written a beautiful, moving book, *Broken Dreams, Fulfilled Promises*,[13] in which she shares a prayer that she and her husband Johan prayed when their son Jozua was desperately ill. Jozua, a tiny baby, was obviously not a prodi-gal, but their prayer of relinquishment is one that we can take to our own hearts and lips. Read the prayer through carefully, so that the decision to make it your own will be a thoughtful one. And if and when we pray that prayer, let us know once more that the Father *is* able to bring the prodigals home — to *his* house.

> *Jesus, he is yours.*
> *First and foremost, he is yours.*
> *We so wanted him as our own.*
> *We so wanted him to grow and find the destiny you*
>   *had for him …*
> *We relinquish our rights to him.*
> *He is yours, first and foremost.*
> *Thank you for the days that You have given him to us*
>   *to enjoy.*
> *Thank you for letting us hear his first gasp of breath.*
> *Thank you for the incredible privilege of co-creating*
>   *with you in a new life.*
> *Even now, his life was not lived in vain.*
> *We were able to see just a little more of your sunshine*
>   *and joy through his birth.*
> *Thank you for allowing us to love him.*
> *Thank you for teaching us to dream dreams that go*
>   *further than just ourselves.*
> *Thank you for the incredible miracle of seeing new life.*
> *But first and foremost, he is yours.*
> *Amen.*

chapter seven

Guilty as Charged?

*Shame is a very heavy feeling. It is a feeling that we do not measure up
and maybe will never measure up to the sorts of people we are meant
to be. The feeling, when we are conscious of it, gives us a vague disgust
with ourselves, which in turn feels like a hunk of lead on our hearts.*

LEWIS SMEDES

ecently I visited the British Houses of Parliament and
gave an address at the National Prayer Breakfast in
the Great Hall of Westminster. A few yards from where I
preached, there is a bronze plaque on the floor. It was on
this very spot, in January 1649, that King Charles I stood before parliament and heard the voices of his gathered accusers.
With narrowed eyes and pointed fingers, they condemned
him as a "tyrant, traitor, murderer and public enemy to the
Commonwealth of England." Charles was brought back to
that same spot over the course of the next few days and finally heard sentence passed: "You shall be put to death by the
severing of your head from your body." His execution took
place just three days later.

I shivered as I stared at that plaque and wondered how it
felt to be so accused; even the king of the realm couldn't get
out of that tight spot.

Those who love prodigals, especially parents, often live in the dock of endless accusation. Convinced that their prodigals' trip to the far country is mainly their fault, they carry around with them a collection of "should haves" and "what ifs." It is a heavy and confusing place to dwell, because usually the guilt that we feel is a mixture of truth and lies; there are some things that we *did* get wrong that should be corrected —but this will invariably be mixed up with false guilt too. When it comes to parenting, friendship, or being a sibling, none of us are all that we could have been—and most of us are not guilty of all that we feel accused of.

Guilty—There Is Only One Perfect One

When a prodigal heads for the bright lights, those left behind are prone to torment themselves with the question, "Did we make mistakes?" That question can be absolutely resolved right here, right now: We all have. There is no such thing as the perfect parent outside of heaven. Jesus acknowledged our shortcomings as human parents when he said, "If you, then, *though you are evil*, know how to give good gifts to your children, how much more will your Father in heaven give good gifts to those who ask him!"[1] There are no friends, parents, or churches that always get it right, all of the time. Relating to others is not an exact science. In the ebb and flow of day-to-day life, words will spill out in haste or thought-lessness; actions will have been taken that we wish now we could undo. We did not surrender our souls to rampant evil when we took that phone call during dinner and so fractured that moment of family sharing; we just answered a ringing phone. No mischief was in our minds when we left for that extended business trip; it put food on the table and was what we felt we had to do at the time. That's not to say we were right. Hindsight may show us that it was not for food that we worked so hard, but for that exotic vacation, which we could have survived without (but which our children enjoyed).

Some of us feel that we were too pushy with our faith, that we should have let that teenager sleep in on Sunday morning and not insisted on a Scripture reading and family prayers at dinner. Others feel the opposite pain: knowing that "one generation will commend your works to another,"[2] we wonder if we neglected our responsibilities. Did we fail to impress the good news upon our children, and so now they have rejected it, perhaps because they think it didn't mean enough to us? Or maybe we expected too much of the youth pastor, who was only with our kids for an hour a week, while days were spent with us.

Did we major on minors when we insisted on that haircut for our son—or were we too liberal? Maybe we didn't insist that they only listen to Christian music, but we didn't anticipate them joining Marilyn Manson's fan club. Is their alcohol problem somehow linked to our enjoyment of wine with meals? Whatever the issue, it comes back to one accusation: their choice to head for the far country was because of *us*, and we are failures. Perhaps all of us feel our shortcomings more keenly than our strengths, and therefore live with ongoing regret. Rob Parsons writes:

> So many parents are carrying a heavy load of guilt they have no right to bear. That's not to say they have been perfect parents. They have just been *parents*—parents who have given this task their very best efforts. There's hardly a mother or father on the face of the earth who wouldn't love to have another shot at parenting—to rewind the clock and get the chance to read all the books

and go to all the seminars before their children hit the teenage years—but even if we had that chance, the truth is we'd probably just make different mistakes.[3]

But some of us are aware that we made significant, major mistakes—and we should humbly take responsibility for them. No time-travel car is currently available to go back in time and undo them, but we can act redemptively today about what we regret from yesterday. Let's not shrug off our guilt too quickly, for as Mark Twain wisely remarked, "It's good to feel guilty when you are." There's a danger that we can write off all guilt as being bad, as does agony Aunt Ann Landers in one column:

> One of the most painful, self mutilating, time and energy consuming exercises in the human experience is guilt. It can ruin your day—or your week or your life—if you let it. It turns up like a bad penny when you do something dishonest, hurtful, tacky, selfish, or rotten ... never mind that it was the result of ignorance, thoughtlessness, weak flesh, or clay feet. You did wrong and the guilt is killing you. Too bad. But be assured, the agony you feel is normal. Remember that guilt is a pollutant and we don't need any more of it in the world.[4]

Wayne Dyer, who wrote the bestseller *Your Erroneous Zones*, joins with the assault to eradicate guilt, quite wrongly declaring guilt to be "the most useless of all erroneous zone behaviors. Guilt zones must be exterminated, spray cleaned and sterilized forever."[5] But this "spray cleaning" will not happen as we honestly repent of our sins and seek forgiveness, according to the new gurus like Dyer. Rather, our salvation comes as we realize that *all* guilt is negative—an idea that is completely at odds with biblical Christianity.

Dyer and Landers are quite wrong. Those who cannot blush with shame are to be pitied, not applauded. Great evils have been perpetuated by those who fought all feelings of guilt like an enemy. Guilt is a gift from God, a hint from heaven that we are more than animals. To be without it is to be psychopathic.

I spend a lot of my life telling people not to be guilty, but sometimes guilt must be accepted. I walk on tiptoe here, but the following must be said. There are some who are reading these words now who know that their children have fled from the Father's house because they have been sexually abused by the very ones with whom they should have been so safe: their parents, grandparents, or wider family members. Perhaps you have been guilty of that sin; please don't close this book right now. I beg you to bring to light what has been buried for too long—to repent, confess, apologize, and take whatever consequences come. Don't rationalize your action or hide behind the insistence that God has forgiven you, so all is well. That prodigal may be waiting for you to flee your far country before they'll begin to think of returning themselves. To deny abuse is to continue to abuse. That denial builds a dark prison house for the abused, a shadowy place where they are forced to eke out their days, surviving rather than living. What was done in the past was bad enough; do not extend the torment further by denial.

And the rest of us need to face our failures honestly too, and work through what always seems to be a surprise: that we have not been right, or done well, all of the time. Rather than wallowing around in speculation or condemnation, we come before God and ask him to show us our shortcomings. And then we do whatever we can to put those failings right, as we not only apologize, but also seek to avoid repeating those errors or slipping into those tendencies. The father in the prodigal story had nothing to apologize for because he represents God, the perfect Father.[6] But the rest of us probably have some work to do. Perhaps a few more prodigals would repent if they saw repentance modeled for them. Are we praying that our prodigals will come home with an apology —when some of them are waiting for us to go to them and honestly say that we are sorry?

Guilty, but Not Shamed

It might be that even now we are thinking of episodes that make us ashamed. We are in a danger zone, a place where good guilt can turn into a smothering blanket of shame and we define ourselves by our worst moments.

We have not been great parents every second, but that reality doesn't make us failed parents. But those searing, memorable episodes can cause us to forget the times when we *did* do well. Michelangelo Buonarroti was one of the greatest artists of all time, a man whose name has become synonymous with the word "masterpiece." As an artist he was unmatched, the creator of works of sublime beauty that express the full breadth of the human condition.

But he was a socially inept, insecure man—the enmity between him and Leonardo da Vinci is famous. And he had episodes of crippling self-doubt and crises of confidence in his own ability. During the painting of "Creation Day" on the ceiling of the Sistine Chapel, he had a particularly difficult day up on the backbreaking scaffolding. That night the great man wrote these words in his journal: "I am not a painter." Temporarily blinded to his own abilities, he forgot the thousands of brilliant moments of genius and sought to place himself on the scrap heap of one difficult day.

As those with regrets, our worst moments scream at us, drowning out the whispers of our triumphs and ultimately causing us to forget them altogether.

Rob Parsons shares a letter from a mother that acknowledges moments of failure, but refuses to forget all the beautiful times:

> You might be surprised to hear from me. It is some time since we spoke, even longer since we were together. But I have rewound and reworded our last conversation and relived our last meeting many times in my heart and imagination.
>
> Words passed between us which would have been best left unsaid. Others could have built bridges across which to reach each other but were dismissed before they ever reached our lips. I painfully regret both.
>
> But not all the memories are painful. I often wind the tape back further like video film and watch you as a child, clambering on a rocky beach, or running with an excited smile to show me some treasure. I can still feel your hand in mine as you urged me to hurry along a windy street or held me back because you wanted to watch a tiny insect on an even slower journey. I remember you as you grew. The challenges you faced and the friends you made. The pride I felt.
>
> Then I wonder when things started to go wrong. When we stopped talking and started shouting. When even the shouting gave way to silence, and the silence to absence.
>
> You have walked a path in these last days that I would not have chosen for you. But, as you often said, it is your life and you must choose for yourself, and I have accepted

those choices, however different they might be from my own.

I want you to know that my love for you is greater than those differences. That despite all that has built a barrier between us, the love I have for you is strong enough to move it, even if piece by piece, and however long it takes.

Both of us need the forgiveness of the other. We still need to hear the words we've longed for. I believe it's never too late.

You may choose to ignore these words. They may make you angry, rekindling memories that you thought you had long forgotten. I understand that. But as your mother I can do nothing but go on loving you, go on asking for your forgiveness, and offering mine to you. No matter what has happened in the past and whatever is going on in your life right now, I love you, I am here for you and you can always come home.[7]

By all means, ask the Lord to show you where you got it wrong yesterday in order to do better today, but most of us need to resist emulating Michelangelo's reckless act, where he temporarily wrote himself off because of his struggles.

Guilty, but Accepting God's Forgiveness

If we sense that God is bringing key episodes of failure to mind, then we should do what we can to put them right with God, and, wherever possible, with those we feel we've failed. And we should accept God's grace for our failures, lest we become those who wrestle with God and argue that we cannot accept his verdict on our failings. C. S. Lewis writes, "I think that if God forgives us we must forgive ourselves.

Otherwise it is almost like setting up ourselves as a higher tribunal than him."

If we endeavor to set up that higher tribunal, we will live in daily torment. And we will become like the character of Rodrigo Mendoza in the film *The Mission*. Robert de Niro plays Mendoza, a deeply flawed man traumatized by guilt. Eventually he agrees, as an act of penance, to accompany a team of Jesuit missionaries on a trip to the Amazon, but he insists on dragging a full suit of armor, tied up in a rope bag and trussed to his back. He just can't bring himself to sever the cord. One of the Jesuits cuts the bag off him during a perilous ascent up a waterfall, but Rodrigo insists on climbing all the way back down to tie the armor bag back on.[8] We do not serve our prodigals well when we are brazen and cavalier about our flaws ("Jesus has forgiven me, so must you"), but neither do we bless them when we insist on lugging around the dead weight of shame. Our praying will be stifled, the light of our hope will flicker and die, and we will be paralyzed rather than mobilized.

We must respond to the redeeming nudge of good guilt and reject the suffocating shame of bad guilt. And some of us must realize that, flawed though we are, we are not ultimately responsible for our prodigal's behavior.

Not Guilty: Even Perfect Parents Have Prodigals

We are responsible for the *input* that we gave our children—but we are not responsible for the *outcome*. They enjoy the gift of free will and are able to choose what they will do with what we have taught them. God's input to Adam and Eve in the garden of Eden was perfect and flawless. He spent time with them, provided for them, gave them opportunity for exploration, dignified them with authority, relaxed them with play—but the outcome, as we well know, was a disaster. Rob Parsons writes:

> What if we could have been the *perfect* parents? The creation story brings a fascinating dimension to this. Adam and Eve had the perfect father and lived in the perfect environment but they chose a way their father didn't want them to go. In fact much of the Bible shows God, the perfect parent, saying to his children, "Why are you turning your back on all that I have taught you?" There are no guarantees with our children.[9]

And as one Seattle-based pastor said:

> Our children are loaned, not given to us, by God. We do our best to raise them to fear and love the Lord, but eventually we have to give them back to him. How they respond to God is not a total reflection on us. We do our best to be faithful, but we can't make their commitment to God for them.[10]

Earlier I mentioned William Wilberforce, the great campaigner against slavery. Despite his incredibly demanding schedule, he managed to give quality time to his children and doted on them. A friend noted that he had a remarkable love for children, and obviously enjoyed their company. It is said that there was a time when his own children were playing upstairs and he was frustrated at having misplaced a letter, when he heard a great din of children shouting. His guest thought he would be frustrated. Instead a great smile formed on his face, and he remarked that, in the midst of a worrying and busy life, that the sound of their voices and the knowledge that they were well, was a delight to him.

He was an unusual father for his day. Most fathers who had the wealth and position he did rarely saw their children. Servants and a governess took care of them, and they were to be out of sight most of the time. Instead, William insisted on eating as many meals as possible with the children, and he joined in their games. He played marbles and blindman's bluff and ran races with them. In the games, the children treated him like one of them.

But when his oldest son, William, was at Trinity College, Oxford, he fell away from the Christian faith. His father agonized; he was fearful that his son would become the plaything of bullies and misled by corrupting influences. In his grief, Wilberforce tried to take his son's spiritual destiny entirely upon his own shoulders, and felt that if only he could serve more, pray more, and love God more, then that would influence a turnaround in his son's heart.

We can always feel that more could have been done. And wisdom is not something that we can force-feed to others. We are not mediators between God and our prodigals—Jesus has already taken that task. Wilberforce successfully changed his world, but like many leaders, struggled because he apparently could not change his son's heart. Leaders can be especially quick to take undue responsibility upon themselves when their children head for the far country. Ironically, most understand that they cannot bear an undue burden for the churches they lead. A minister can teach and preach well, serve selflessly, and care for the people in his or her church with genuine love—and still see spiritual or moral failure in that church. But the minister cannot accept responsibility for the personal failures of that congregation. The apostle Paul invested in the church at Corinth, and despite all his efforts, it was a divided church. There was immorality and abuse of the Lord's Supper. But Paul did not walk away from the church wringing his hands and saying, "Where did I go wrong?" Instead of writing a letter detailing his failures, he addressed their issues. Our self-flagellation might not even lead us to anything positive. Ironically, the destabilizing effects of false guilt can make us worse, rather than better, in our relationships. Parents, driven by guilt that doesn't belong to them, give money when they shouldn't, agree to compromises that are inappropriate, and can spend years trying to pay back for the perceived failures.

With all of our flaws and failures, we are greatly loved—and outrageously forgiven. We need to grasp that truth and live in the good of it, lest our days be eclipsed with irrational sadness and we cease to pray.

> *Lord,*
> *I have only ever loved her.*
> *You know how that feels. To give a child everything and*
>   *watch them throw it all away.*
> *Sometimes the guilt causes me to cry myself to sleep,*
> *and when I wake it is in my stomach.*
> *I rewind the past and ask, "What could we have done?"*
> *Or sometimes, "What if I hadn't . . . ?"*
> *I watch others who are proud, sometimes, it seems, even*
>   *boastful of their children,*
> *Although I would not rob them of a moment of their*
>   *pleasure.*
> *Cut me free from what others might think or say.*
> *From the pain of hearing them congratulate themselves for*
>   *the way their children have "turned out."*
> *As if the mold she has fallen from was a "second."*
> *Help me find a place with those who understand and have*
>   *known this pain.*

I need you to whisper to me that I did my best,
I was not perfect but I gave what I could.
And, Lord, even where I failed you can mend.
If I wounded, you can heal.
Heal me, Lord.
Lift this guilt.
Now.[11]

chapter eight

Praying for the Prodigals

> *Do not worry about "proper" praying,*
> *just talk to God.*
> **RICHARD FOSTER**

*G*od wants us to pray for the prodigals. Prayer cries out for protection for those in a dangerous land, summons the winning influence of the Spirit that can soften a calloused heart, and lights up a pathway home. Surely our petitions can pave stepping-stones back to the Father's house.

But why should we pray? Surely God could just go right ahead and directly turn fugitives from Christ into his followers once more. And then, what is prayer, and what form should our praying take—what if our methods or approach to prayer are wrong? Will our prodigals stay in twilight because we failed them in prayer? The old enemy that we considered in the last chapter, guilt, stalks us. Now we are bowed low by a double burden: not only are we failures in our *horizontal* relationships, as bad parents, siblings, or friends, but our *vertical* relationship with God doesn't seem too good either. And ironically, those twin punches of guilt mean that we pray less—what's the point of laboring in prayer when enough is never enough and our labors will always be in vain? To the statement "I am not a good parent/friend/sibling," we add another self-indictment: *I am not an effective Christian.*

Why Pray?

God is the executive producer and director of the universe. He didn't make it and move on; he continues to act, influence, call, and intervene by the second. His mission is to bring his loving rule (the shorthand word for that is "kingdom") to every aspect and corner of creation—including bringing home the prodigals.

But his moment-by-moment involvement with everything is shaped and influenced by prayer. This is God's way. He has decided to harness the involvement of numerous "associate directors" onto the movie set that is life, to partner with him today and every day. In truth, it is both a frustration—and a wonder—that God has determined to work his works through partnership with his people. Here is awesome and bewildering news: *we* are those associate directors.

The mystery of the Trinity shows us that God has never been an independent operator: the community of God that is Father, Son, and Spirit reveals a team of persons at the heart of all that there is. The call to pray is the winsome invitation to join God (not to become as gods) in the direction of his creation. So it is that prayer is such a vital key to seeing prodigals find their rest and home in God; the Lord could woo them without our petitions but generally chooses not to do so. Here we see the incredible dignity and potential that God has invested in human beings; we are summoned to step up, survey the landscape, and by our praying, affect the terrain.

"Proper" Praying

Although they are often not aware of it themselves, those who love prodigals are usually rather good at prayer—at least that which constitutes prayer in God's eyes. It isn't that they are skilled with stringing words together and can make long, articulate speeches for heaven's benefit. In fact, their words might be few. They may struggle to weave together words that express their feelings, and may hesitate to pray out loud during a public prayer gathering.

And it isn't that they are natural hermits who can spend hours, days, or weeks in focused intercession. In truth, they may not spend long in concentrated "prayer" (as we popularly know it) at all.

They may not be granted great revelations, or report intricate conversations with God or his angels.

But despite all of the above, those who love prodigals are usually gifted in prayer, because they have hearts that are broken. Just as Hannah sobbed out her desperate plea for the child that she had never known,[1] so there are many others who agonize for the children that they have known, but now seem to know no longer.

Prayer is simply about being with God. Just as human intimacy can be expressed in a myriad of ways—a look, a sigh, a touch, a knowing nod, and words too—so prayer can include the hours spent hoping; the acts of service, kindness, and forgiveness; the fears shared with God and the tears shed before him. Susan Lenzkes writes, "Pain is a language, without words—and so it is untouched by words ... my prayers for you are often wordless too ... and shaped like tears."[2] In a sense, there is no such act as "proper" praying. Prayer might be worrying out loud in God's direction, muttering our brief thanks for a tiny breakthrough, or pounding the floor with frustration. It is conversation, the sharing of the stuff of everyday life in everyday language. As a father, I love to hear the sound of my children's voices, and speech-making from them would not only be unwelcome, but offensive.

A commitment to simplicity prevents us from making the same mistakes as the Pharisees, who, in Jesus' day, prayed at volume on the street corners. These trained experts in public prayer were required to intercede for a minimum of three hours each day. They were convinced that the only *good* praying was *long* praying—but Jesus links their wide open mouths with their inflated egos: The teachers of the law "for a show make lengthy prayers."[3] In the evangelical subculture, a similar idea still exists today, even if only at a subconscious level. If you're going to pray, it had better be for at least an hour. And while it *is* good to set quality time aside to spend with God, the bitter irony is that often, because we feel that we can't pray for an hour, we don't pray at all, and we miss the golden opportunity for genuinely helpful moments spent consciously with God. Isn't it better to *pray* for five minutes than to *aspire to pray* for an hour (and indeed passionately believe that hour-long praying is the way to go), but not pray at all? If we have this "never mind the quality, feel the width" approach to prayer, then we miss out on the opportunity of just being with Jesus and sharing our joys and struggles with him.

Prayer As Voodoo

Some of us treat prayer like some kind of voodoo charm. We pray, perhaps even backing up our pleading with fasting, and look for a swift, satisfying result. But then there is nothing. We spy no welcome sight of a returning prodigal on the horizon, and so the answer hasn't come, at least in our estimation. God must be deaf to our cries, blind to our tears, unable or unwilling to act at our desperate bidding. We are angry. And we are quite wrong.

Prayer is not a kind of control mechanism, magic in Jesus' name. We are calling for change in someone who has their own willpower, their own choices to make, and our praying doesn't override or cancel out that reality. Our prayers call for kind, loving influences to surround our prodigals, but they have the choice to welcome or shun those influences. Our prayers cry out for depraved and deceptive voices to be stilled, but the prodigal may still tune in to satanic whispers if she chooses.

And then who are we to judge if our praying is effective? A friend often reminds me that most of what God does, he does behind our backs. But we might assume that our prayers are not being answered because we see no *visible* fruit of our praying. But we have absolutely no knowledge of those secret moments, known only to the prodigal and their God. We are absolutely unaware of the conscience that troubles them, their restless nights, their developing boredom with "fun" that has become hollow and tedious, and their conversations about God with people we've never met, and never will meet.

I know of one couple who had the most extreme experience of prodigality with their daughter, who dabbled with drugs and the occult. They then discovered shocking evidence that their own daughter was making plans to murder them. She was angry and hateful, all the outward signs were hopeless. But something greater was happening within the heart of the troubled young woman. She attended a youth retreat, came home, and simply announced, "I've changed."

They never found out what happened during that retreat and never pressed her, but this was no flash-in-the-pan youth camp commitment. Their daughter rediscovered the smile that she had lost for years, and new affection and respect came into her relationship with her parents and brother. She wrote in a journal, "All of us should live life so as to be able to face eternity at any time."

That journal entry was to be tested. That young woman was Cassie Bernall, who found herself facing the two fellow students—and gunmen—who stormed Columbine High School on April 20, 1999.[4] One of them challenged Cassie with a straightforward, confrontational question: "Do you believe in God?" She said yes, and they shot her dead. The teenager who had once plotted the death of her own parents had become a faithful witness for Christ—a martyr. Her parents were never to know the full details of the long journey that took her to that bravest of days, her final moment. But she took the journey nonetheless.

No wonder we're told to "pray and not give up."[5] Prayer is truly a campaign of warfare, a lengthy battle rather than a brief skirmish.

Some Words for Those Lost for Words

So prayer is more than words, just as love is more than a kiss. Yet prayer includes words, which presents some of us with a dilemma: when it comes to *speaking* to God about our prodigals, where do we start? I confess that sometimes I don't talk to God more because *I simply can't think of anything useful to say.* As someone from a church background that didn't include or value liturgy (and at times derided it), I have discovered that to take the carefully shaped words of another—words that are the fruit of meditation and reflection and that, therefore, leap and dance with biblical truth, words that have been the comfort of believers through the centuries—has added another dimension to my spirituality.

Some of us are averse to liturgy, claiming that repetition itself is lifeless. We write off any form of liturgy as sanctified script-reading from an ancient and modern autocue. But think again: surely it is *vain* repetition that is the problem. The words that flow from another's experience and heart may give us a vocabulary to express something so deep and overwhelming for which we are unable to find a language of our own.

With that in mind, will you allow me to offer you what is at best a flawed attempt at a simple prayer for our prodigals? Use it if it helps, not as a mindless mantra, but perhaps as an act of love at the dawning and the dusk of each day. At times, when you use this prayer, you might choose to light a candle, its warm glow symbolizing hope.

> *Loving heavenly Father,*
> *I come as I am, hoping for hope, faith-filled or faithless, to*
>   *pray for _____.*
> *Loose their hands, and link their hands.*
> *Open their eyes, to evil, and to love.*
> *Clear their minds, to see where they are, and where they*
>   *should be.*
> *Soften their hearts to your love, and may their faith not fail.*
> *Direct their feet toward your own pathways.*
> *Wrap your protection around them, blessed Trinity.*
> *They are yours.*
> *Please bring them home to you.*
> *I pray in the strong, powerful name of Jesus Christ.*
> *Amen.*

Words only become significant as we pause and consider their meaning, so let's take some time to ponder the background to that prayer. If you decide to regularly make the prayer your own, then revisit these discussions from time to time.

We Come to Our Father As We Are

Loving heavenly Father, I come as I am, hoping for hope, faith-filled or faithless ...

Fatherhood is not optional in relationship to our spirituality; Jesus insists in his teaching that we use the language of family when we come to God in prayer. When we approach God, he will not let us be content with addressing him as Lord, King, Sovereign, Creator—or even simply as God. He is, of course, all of the above, and yet insists on being *more* to us than all of these. To come to him as merely God or Lord is to enter into dialogue with him on the basis of his *power* and the extent of his reign—but makes no reference to his *relationship* to us and ours to him. But every single time we use the word "Father" we celebrate and remind ourselves that we are his and he, ours. Every prayer becomes another family reunion. And the insistence that we call him "Father" takes us beyond the God-as-my-vending-machine mechanics that can characterize some praying, and draws us once again not just to the Potentate of Potentates (though that he surely is) but to a warm bosom of love. He simply will not let us shout our prayers from a distance. Every time we utter his name, we remember that we are home and that we are his children.

Once our family relationship has been established, our calling him "Father" also reminds us that we come to One who has power to change things and give wise insight from his vantage point. As children, we are freely invited to bring our requests without hesitation. Again, this flies in the face of our human experience, where we might have been scolded by our human parents because of our incessant begging for yet another candy bar or another unneeded toy. And yet we serve a God whose only complaints in this respect seem to be about our *not* asking, or when our asking has an obsessive selfishness at its heart. "When you ask, you do not receive, because you ask with wrong motives, that you may spend what you get on your pleasures."[6] The invitation and command to come to him as Father establishes a protocol of communication — neither the distant, formal speech-making that one might use when addressing a king, nor the chumminess that one might use with a pal. Our privilege is to know intimacy without flippancy.

And all of this is because of grace. Robert Farrar Capon points out that God is Father, not Santa Claus; he is not like the character in the dreadful Christmas song "Santa Claus Is Coming to Town," who is "making a list, he's checking it twice, he's going to find out who's naughty or nice." Capon elaborates:

> Jesus ... is not, thank God, Santa Claus. He will come to the world's sins with no list to check, no tests to grade, no debts to collect, no scores to settle. He will wipe away the handwriting that was against us and nail it to his cross (Col. 2:14). He will save, not some minuscule coterie of good little boys and girls with religious money in their piggy banks, but all the stone broke, deadbeat, over extended children of the world whom He, as the Son of Man — the Holy Child of God, the ultimate big kid, if you please — will set free in the liberation of his death

... he tacks a "Gone Fishing" sign over the sweatshop of religion, and for all the debts of all sinners who ever lived, he provided the exact change for free. How nice it would be if the church could only remember to keep itself in on the joke.[7]

The fatherhood of God is the basis for our confidence in prayer, and it's the celebration message the world is quite literally dying to hear. I like Capon's analogy of the "joke." How wonderful it will be when more of those deeply saddened and depressed by Satan's morose trinkets hear the infectious sound of our salvation laughter. And the fatherhood of God is the reason we can pray for our prodigals today—because, ultimately, whatever our relationship with them, *he* is their Father, and he cares deeply about their not being home. And he feels our pain as we watch that empty horizon, for he is *our* Father too. And as our Father, he is well aware of our multiple weaknesses.

We come as we are. We are all flawed and in process. If we wait until we feel that we have arrived before we pray, then we will never pray—it's as simple as that. The wonderful news that God will never love us any more or less than he does at this very second is both glorious and difficult to grasp. Karl Barth, the world-famous theologian, arrived at the University of Chicago to deliver some lectures and was asked by the press what the most profound truth was that he had learned in all his years of study. Barth thought for a moment and then responded: "The deepest and most profound truth that I have ever discovered is this: Jesus loves me, this I know, for the Bible tells me so."

But it is one thing to discover the truth, and another to live in the good of that revelation. Like the prodigal, wrestling in the hug of his father and desperate to still deliver his "I'm not worthy to be called your son, make me like one of your hired servants" speech, many of us resist the idea of outrageous grace poured out on *us*. We are the descendants of super-wrestler Jacob, whose prayer was "I will not let you go unless you bless me."[8] But our wrestling turns his prayer around on its head: "I will not let you bless me; let me go."

It is not that we do not believe that God loves; rather we are not convinced that God can love *us* that much.

A missionary—and missionaries are obviously known for their high levels of commitment to and sacrifices for Jesus—wrote of her lingering feeling that the God who loves the world might stop short of liking her:

> Our inability to develop a truly God-shaped set of expectations easily could leave us wandering out the forty years or so of our adult lives in our own self-made desert wilderness. In my case, the greatest consequence of long-term, misplaced expectations has been their deadening effect on spiritual vitality. I questioned God, myself, my circumstances ....God must not love me the way He loves others, I thought. I must be on Jesus' blacklist. I guess I'm just one of those Christians that God can't use.[9]

We come to pray for prodigals, with all their issues, knowing that we have lots of issues of our own, which I hope we are gradually working through. Without that awareness, we descend into being the pious ones waiting for the lesser specimens of grace to clean up. Jesus rejected the man praying who believed that he was better than others, but he accepted the prayers of the humble man who felt overwhelmed by his sinfulness.[10] So we come to pray, not qualified to petition God for any other reason than that he has bid us come.

The familiar and beautiful words of the hymn "Just As I Am" have impacted millions across the world—some say the hymn has had more effect than any other. The composer, Charlotte Elliott, had lived a happy life in Brighton, England. Known as "Carefree Charlotte," she was a popular portrait artist and a writer of humorous verse. At the age of thirty, however, a serious illness disabled her for life and she became listless and depressed. A visit from a well-known evangelist changed her thinking—and she realized that she was welcome before God, with all her struggles and pains. The hymn was the fruit of that life change. We can make its lovely stanzas our own:

> *Just as I am, without one plea*
> *But that thy blood was shed for me*
> *And that thou bidd'st me come to thee*
> *O Lamb of God, I come, I come.*
>
> *Just as I am, though tossed about*
> *With many a conflict, many a doubt,*
> *Fightings and fears within, without,*
> *O Lamb of God, I come, I come.*
>
> *Just as I am, poor, wretched, blind;*
> *Sight, riches, healing of the mind,*
> *Yea, all I need, in Thee to find,*
> *O Lamb of God, I come, I come.*
>
> *Just as I am, Thou wilt receive,*
> *wilt welcome, pardon, cleanse, relieve;*
> *because Thy promise I believe,*
> *O Lamb of God, I come! I come!*[11]

Relationships

Loose their hands, and link their hands.

Humans run in herds—none of us are original. The fashion and music industries would not flourish as they do if it

were not for the fact that the majority of us are conform-
ists. We like to fit in, and, ironically, those who reject trend,
custom, and culture are dubbed eccentric. Anyone who has
parented teenagers knows the power of peer pressure. Our
prodigals are the product of their relationships, both positively and negatively. As the ever-blunt apostle Paul puts
it, "Bad company corrupts character."[12] Scripture is littered
with the stories of those who got into serious trouble because
they got in with the wrong crowd. Scripture warns us not to
be "carried away" by bad influencers.[13] Solomon, renowned
for his wisdom, tripped up because of his foreign wives; his
latter years were sullied by idolatry because they "turned his
heart after other gods."[14] His son, Rehoboam, chose younger
advisors rather than the trusted elders—with disastrous
results.[15] Compare their drifting with the golden reign of
David (who himself was obviously not without serious flaw),
but whose intention was to make sure that he did not come
under the influence of evildoers:

> Men of perverse heart shall be far from me;
>   I will have nothing to do with evil.
> Whoever slanders his neighbor in secret,
>   him will I put to silence;
> whoever has haughty eyes and a proud heart,
>   him will I not endure.
> My eyes will be on the faithful in the land,
>   that they may dwell with me;
> he whose walk is blameless
>   will minister to me.
> No one who practices deceit
>   will dwell in my house.
> no one who speaks falsely
>   will stand in my presence.[16]

As we ask for hands to be loosed, we are praying against the dark influences of negative friendships. It is not that we are calling for those unhelpful friends to be consigned to outer darkness, but rather we are calling to break the unhealthy hold that friendships and relationships can create. Users can attach themselves to prodigals like magnets, and then prove to be fair-weather friends when life gets tough. We pray that those users and losers will loose their grip upon those we love.

And positively, we ask that the hands of our prodigals be linked with those who would love, help, confront, and care for them, and who would bring a wholesome influence to bear upon their lives. Just as the newly converted Saul was nurtured and cared for by that patient and master of encouragement, Barnabas,[17] so we pray for people who will tend and love those who right now would spurn our loving attention.

Warfare

Open their eyes, to evil, and to love.

It seemed like such a delightful movie, and I enthused about it for days. As someone with a pathological hatred for cold, sterile religion, I was briefly converted—perhaps seduced is a better word—by the magical world of *Chocolat*. In this movie, there is no menacing evil, no gratuitous violence or explicit sex. *Good Housekeeping* magazine described it as "a witty plea for passion and pleasure against repression and denial."

Vianne is a single mom who relocates to a staunchly Catholic village in France and opens a chocolate store, which is filled with mouth-watering delights and fragranced by the selfless kindness and welcome that she offers to all. She stands out as a winsome figure of beauty, surrounded by the small-minded, repressed villagers, who are all dressed in black. They never smile, and they are all under the control of the legalistic, repressive mayor, but Vianne refuses to bow the knee. She is easy to love, with her nonconformist refusal to join in with the dirge that is Mass, and her giggly pursuit of happiness. At the end of the film, the Catholic priest delivers a sermon that is testimony to his converting to the "freedom" of religion that is Vianne's. We cheer (or I did) as he throws off the shackles of religion and denial.

Sharing dinner with some friends a few days later, I enthused about the movie and was a little taken aback when our hostess told me flatly how angry the film made her, and how it was just a con. And as I listened to her reasoning, I realized that she was totally right, and that I had been suckered. I had swallowed the film's blatant message of hedonism, which always leads to despair, because the message was so well disguised, at least to this poor chap who apparently lacks any measurable discernment. In *Chocolat*, any and all choices are valid—except the decision to be a follower of Christ. And the Christianity that is mocked is a straw target anyway. Genuine, authentic Christianity—far from perpetuating lifeless, cold religion—turns both barrels onto the frigid piety of the Pharisees. Jesus was bolder in his denunciation of their brand of piety than the gorgeous chocolate vendor. But my point is this: I was taken in because sin was so well disguised. It nearly always is.

Sin is such an obviously bad deal, so it has to come sugar- or chocolate-coated. Scripture describes the Enemy as a brilliant tactician (although he tends to use the same old techniques repeatedly), subtle and wily. Temptation's source is one who wants to "have" our prodigals and establish his dark mastery over their lives. And so we pray that they will see through the candy coating and realize that squirming worms infest the rotten apple.

Satan is one who would blind the eyes of the prodigals and leave them fumbling around in confusion and darkness.[18] So we pray that God will open their eyes to see the deceitfulness of sin and to reject its madness.

And then, once again, we pray for eyes to be widened to the winsome love of God, that false caricatures that malign him will erode, that their memories will remind them of answered prayer and acts of divine kindness in their past. Prodigals are often very nostalgic, and for good reason: life really is better with God at the center. We pray that God will remind them of the warmth and security that they felt in his arms.

Thinking: Mind and Heart

Clear their minds, to see where they are, and where they should be. Soften their hearts to your love, and may their faith not fail.

In the prodigal parable, the wayward son had a revelation—about his own condition. Surely part of sin's deception is that we attempt to tell ourselves that life is great, when in fact it might be numbingly dull and empty. The college student who downs a lethal cocktail of beer and shots spends the night vomiting into a filthy toilet, and then awakes with a splitting headache, may well tell himself that he really is living the high life—how else would and could he do exactly the same thing, with precisely the same results, the following weekend?

But the prodigal "came to" himself. His working conditions were awful and the food nauseating. His friends had vanished and he saw their betrayal clearly. And that nostalgia that I mentioned earlier kicked in—although it was longing for a good, hot meal that tormented him rather than the warmth of relationship in his father's house.

We pray for more than sorrow over their condition. Steve and Sherri knew that there were many times when Craig lamented the state of his life—but that sadness never became an engine to propel him to make good choices about God. Some of us are quite like Judas, who was "seized with remorse" about his betrayal of Christ,[19] but that sadness didn't lead to any repentant decisions. Sorrow can be but a schoolmaster that leads us in the direction of repentance, so Paul speaks to his friends in Corinth about sorrow that leads to repentance.[20] But we are praying for more than tears; we call for the heart-based revolution that is literally a change of mind—and thereafter, a change of behavior.

And we pray especially for their faith, even if it seems to us that there are but dying embers of it left, or that the flame of faith has died altogether. Jesus knew that Peter would become a prodigal and that there was warfare going on—Satan wanted to "sift [him] as wheat."[21] Jesus did not pray that the battle would not happen—perhaps there was a refining work that could only be accomplished if headstrong, self-assured Peter had to walk the shadowy pathway of failure—but he prayed that Peter's faith would not collapse under the pressure of that attack.

Destiny

Direct their feet toward your own pathways.

Some have noticed that when there is a specific call of God upon a person's life (and let us not limit vocational "calling" to the clergy here, for God calls architects, bankers, doctors, nurses, relief workers, and homemakers) and when that destiny is revealed, the battle gets hotter. Notice that it was immediately after the calling and destiny of Jesus had been affirmed from his Father in heaven that battle really commenced in the wilderness.[22] We pray that through good choices the prodigals will come home, not only to relationship with the Lord, but to reconnection with the plan that God has for them.

Protection in the Name

Wrap your protection around them, blessed Trinity. They are yours. Please bring them home to you. I pray in the strong, powerful name of Jesus Christ. Amen.

We end our prayer with a call of love mingled with a statement of release. We express our deeply felt fears as we plead with God to protect them in dangerous territory; yet we realize in our desire to protect, we must not step back into control. They are God's and we ask that they come back to God himself. And our use of the name of Christ is far more than a way of signaling to God that our prayer time is at a close. As we take that name upon our lips, we remind ourselves that this is the ground of our authority. We ask what might seem implausible and even impossible, in the name that beat death, in the name that hell fears, and in the name that has offered us shelter. It is the name that demons cannot argue with; it is the name that enables a rotting corpse that was Lazarus to walk out of his grave and step into the light of life once more.

And ponder that sight: if prayer for your prodigal seems hopeless and vain, then remember that Lazarus, who stank of far worse than the pigpen, was to sit around the table with Jesus once more.[23] This is what encourages us to pray—and to prepare a party too.

chapter nine

Preparing the Party

Warm up the sky, warm up the sky
light a welcoming fire for him . . .
TIM FINN AND NEIL FINN

The parable of the prodigal son involved not only a homecoming, but a lavish party with it. The menu included the choicest veal cuts. The returned son was dolled up in the priciest glad rags, a fine robe draped around his thin shoulders, his bruised feet encased now in luxurious leather sandals. He wore an expensive ring for a party favor. But the happy occasion was not without its tensions. Jesus' story included some familial conflict too, as the elder brother angrily exploded. Coming in from a long, hard day in the fields, he was incensed to hear the strains of music and dancing, offended by the sounds of whooping and laughter in the old house.

The party that the father threw for his young son is a very important element to the parable. It was that party, not the prodigal's decision to come home, that prompted the elder brother to fly off the handle. And the fact that Jesus colored in this wonderful detail in his word portrait of his Father and ours is significant. As we hear the father defending the expense and the noise with the phrase "we *had* to celebrate," we see the wonderful truth that joy, welcome, and acceptance are not optional extras where God is involved. The breathtaking truth is this—there is a party planner at the heart of the universe; this is how he welcomes *his* returning prodigals. And he calls us to be like him. For some of us, this means that we consider what it will mean if that one who has walked away from our home comes back again: how shall we welcome them? And for *all* of us, we have to ask what kind of reception we will give to prodigals that are looking again for God, and have come to us to help them on their way.

He Is the Party Planner

For some Christians, the image of a party is negative. Let's face it, parties can be occasions of excess, where too much alcohol dulls the minds of usually sensible people and mad choices are made in that fog. But, risky though it might seem to some, God loves the imagery of a good party and consistently uses it in the inspired words of Scripture to point to his own nature and the reality that he calls his people to be a partying people.

The festivals of the Old Testament era were huge parties that wonderfully disrupted the working life of Israel as the people of God were called together to toast their love for God and for each other. The book of Deuteronomy includes a command that seems almost unlikely, it is such an invitation to unbridled joy:

> Exchange your tithe for silver, and take the silver with you and go to the place the LORD your God will choose. Use the silver to buy whatever you like: cattle, sheep,

wine or other fermented drink, or anything you wish. Then you and your household shall eat there in the presence of the LORD your God and rejoice.[1]

Here the Party Planner commands his people to celebration, but with the words *anything you wish* allows them space to decide the specific elements of the party. And God himself is not the wallflower, the stoic, unsmiling spectator or party pooper who sits every dance out, because he is above that kind of thing.

Zephaniah, described by one commentator as the prophet obsessed with doom, pictures God as the one who skips and pirouettes for joy over his people. The NIV almost loses the sheer exuberance of it all: "The LORD your God is with you, he is mighty to save. He will take great delight in you, he will quiet you with his love, he will rejoice over you with singing."[2] The Hebrew word used here, translated "rejoice" means "to leap." Just as the father in the prodigal story jumps up and rushes out to meet his son — and running was not considered appropriately dignified behavior for an older man in Hebrew culture — so God is portrayed as One who is not afraid to express his emotion.

Jesus introduced the story of the lost son with a statement often misunderstood: "In the same way, I tell you, there is rejoicing in the presence of the angels of God over one sinner who repents."[3] Often it is preached that it is the angels that are doing all the celebrating, whereas this is not what this verse actually says. Rather it is in "the presence of the angels" that this joy breaks out, surely a reference to the central person in the royal court of heaven, our God himself. And then, in the series of three stories about things that got lost — a sheep, a coin, and a much-loved son — each of them includes not only the recovery of those items, but a celebratory party that followed. The sheep is found, and "when he finds it, he joyfully puts it on his shoulders and goes home. Then he calls his friends and neighbors together and says, 'Rejoice with me; I have found my lost sheep.'"[4] And then the coin is recovered, "and when she finds it, she calls her friends and neighbors together and says, 'Rejoice with me; I have found my lost coin.'"[5] One might almost think that to throw a party over the recovery of a coin is a little extravagant. Some suggest that the coin was the equivalent of her wedding ring. But the One who took the rather unusual step of beginning his ministry at a party (and the staggering step of making his first miracle the mass production of rather fine wine) insists on using the party analogy. Asked what the kingdom of heaven was like, he replied that it was like a party.

> Jesus spoke to them again in parables, saying: "The kingdom of heaven is like a king who prepared a wedding banquet for his son. He sent his servants to those who had been invited to the banquet to tell them to come, but they refused to come.
>
> "Then he sent some more servants and said, 'Tell those who have been invited that I have prepared my dinner: My oxen and fattened cattle have been butchered, and everything is ready. Come to the wedding banquet.'
>
> "But they paid no attention and went off—one to his field, another to his business. The rest seized his servants, mistreated them and killed them. The king was enraged. He sent his army and destroyed those murderers and burned their city.
>
> "Then he said to his servants, 'The wedding banquet is ready, but those I invited did not deserve to come. Go to the street corners and invite to the banquet anyone you find.' So the servants went out into the streets and gath-

ered all the people they could find, both good and bad, and the wedding hall was filled with guests.

"But when the king came in to see the guests, he noticed a man there who was not wearing wedding clothes. 'Friend,' he asked, 'how did you get in here without wedding clothes?' The man was speechless.

"Then the king told the attendants, 'Tie him hand and foot, and throw him outside, into the darkness, where there will be weeping and gnashing of teeth.'

"For many are invited, but few are chosen."[6]

Jesus did not just use the analogy of the party in his *teaching*, but was roundly criticized for *attending* parties. Those who hated Jesus especially homed in on his love of eating and drinking with the wrong crowd: "The Son of Man came eating and drinking, and you say, 'Here is a glutton and a drunkard, a friend of tax collectors and "sinners." ' "[7] And the future to come? It's described as a great party. "Then the angel said to me, 'Write: "Blessed are those who are invited to the wedding supper of the Lamb!" ' "[8] Little wonder that Tony Campolo has used the term "party deity" to describe our awesome God.

The Party: Radical Compassion

But Jesus' description of the celebration feast for the prodigal is more than a wonderful reminder about the nature of God—it is also a loaded statement (one writer calls it a weapon) that blew apart accepted ideas in his day about what true holiness was. Jesus chose to eat and drink with those described as sinners throughout his ministry. One writer describes "table fellowship" as the central feature of his life. Who were these "sinners" with whom he spent so much time? We read our New Testament thinking into the parable and are aghast at the Pharisees' assertion that he "ate with sinners." Who do they think they are—aren't we all sinners? But the Pharisees had not read the book of Romans and so their description of "sinners" meant the pariahs, the social outcasts of the day, those who had chosen one of the seven despised occupations—including tax collectors, those suspected of immorality, and the people who didn't observe the Torah as the Pharisees understood it. "Sinners" was also the term reserved for Gentiles, but table fellowship with Gentiles was not a central feature of Jesus' activity. Obviously Jesus was in the habit of hanging out with the hopeless rejects whose reprobate lifestyles had gotten them into a serious mess.

The character in the prodigal parable was one of those. Jesus painted a word portrait of a young man who had surely gone down to the depths. It was bad enough that he had treated his father like a dead man and stomped off to the far country. But then, when things went bad, he continued to make dreadful choices. Instead of seeking help from a distant synagogue, he got himself a job working for a Gentile, who would have made no provisions for Jewish customs. So the prodigal was portrayed as a Sabbath-breaker. And then look at his choice of a job: he was a swineherd, working with pigs, the most unclean animals in Jewish thinking.

The prodigal didn't just mess up once—he was guilty of multiple profanities, which is perhaps why the father in the story describes him as one thought of as dead, the description usually given of a Jew who had ceased to be a Jew. Jesus builds a profile of a despicable down-and-out, a serial sinner. And this was the guest of honor at a party thrown for him by an ecstatic dad. People like these were welcome at the table where Jesus sat too.

What is the significance of all of this?

In Near Eastern culture, sitting together with another person at a table implied intimacy and fellowship; it was an act of honor, trust, and acceptance. But the Pharisees had sharpened the significance of the table into being a place of religious as well as social significance. The Pharisees were obsessed with the politics and etiquette of eating. Out of 341 rabbinic texts attributed to the Pharisees, 229 of them are rules about eating—so much so that one scholar describes them as a table fellowship sect.[9] They worried about the ritual preparation of food and how the cooked meal was to be eaten. Had tithes been paid on the meat that was to be prepared? Were people present at the table who would defile the occasion? Had proper preparations been made in terms of hand washing, which was more about ceremony than hygiene?

> Then some Pharisees and teachers of the law came to Jesus from Jerusalem and asked, "Why do your disciples break the tradition of the elders? They don't wash their hands before they eat!"
>
> Jesus replied, "And why do you break the command of God for the sake of your tradition?"[10]

The table for the Pharisees represented the solidarity of Israel as a people occupied by hated Gentiles. To share that table with "outsiders" or those who did not take their religion seriously (and who thus threatened to usher the judgment of God upon the nation) was more than socially awkward—in their eyes, it was tantamount to national betrayal, like a

Jewish Frenchman throwing banquets for Nazis in occupied France during the last World War.

The table was also a symbol of their future hope, of the banquet to come, where God would feast with his chosen people. So why did Jesus apparently choose to ride roughshod over all these cherished traditions? The answer is important for us as we think about celebrating with those who are coming back to God: the Pharisees had corrupted the truth about holiness and slammed the door in the faces of the sick people who most needed a physician to heal them.

Jesus was throwing a party of care and compassion. For the Pharisees, holiness had become something that was more about principle than people—separation rather than association. Jesus turned their notion of holiness upside down, first of all calling them to compassion. Surely he was teaching and demonstrating that true holiness will always be compassionate. So in the parable of the good Samaritan, the Samaritan who went to the rescue did so because he had compassion—and Jesus tells us to act in the same manner.[11] What is the driving force that makes the running father in the prodigal story sprint? He has *compassion* on his returning son.[12] Twice in Matthew's gospel,[13] Jesus paraphrases and quotes Hosea, who insists that when it comes to piety, God is looking for more than religious ritualism: "For I desire mercy, not sacrifice, and acknowledgment of God rather than burnt offerings." "Holiness" that can never throw a party of caring welcome for the prodigals is no holiness at all.

We must throw parties of welcome. But what should be on the menu? Angels on archways and specially-built chapels are unnecessary, but there are some other essentials.

The Gift of Readiness —
a Party, but *Not* Planned

When prodigals decide to head toward God, and sometimes toward us, often they don't call ahead or make an appointment. Their return may have been much hoped for, but it is often unanticipated. Everyone has a life with priorities and a schedule, and suddenly that perhaps carefully planned rhythm is wonderfully shattered by a glorious disruption, but a disruption nonetheless. And as we'll see in a moment, a homecoming does not signal the end of the long journey, but heralds the beginning of another phase of travel. The quiet life that you resigned yourself to may have felt empty, but as you are suddenly catapulted back into the intensity of nursing someone in their first faltering steps with God, and perhaps away from addictions and life-threatening habits, there will be moments when that quieter life will look very attractive.

I've discovered that some churches and church leaders don't want to mess with prodigals. Returning prodigals sometimes smell bad, ask awkward questions, are time consuming, and have a tendency to mess up time and time again. I recently spoke at a conference that was dedicated to building "prodigal-friendly churches." One minister sent an email expressing his total disinterest in the conference. He angrily demanded to be removed from any future mailings and emphatically stated that he and his church had no desire to see any prodigals returning to their church. Incredibly, he told us that he was glad that they were gone. I was stunned by his assertion that the return of any prodigals would be awkward for his church, as they would have to buy more chairs.

Parties cost money, time, energy, and there's always a mess to clean up. We must face that challenge and be willing to pay that price, lest we nurse romantic notions about what a "party" might look like.

Interest — The Father Was Looking Out for His Son

When prodigals come back to God, it is important that someone notices their return. However we express it, perhaps the greatest gift that we can give any returning prodigal is the blessing of significance — the message that they matter. Isn't a party thrown in someone's honor really just a delightful mechanism to make a statement that they count? "We're glad that you are alive and we gather to celebrate that fact." We raise a toast to you. Ravi Zacharias describes the need that we all have to matter to someone — particularly to our parents.

> A few years ago, a former Olympic athlete came to visit me. He was looking for some direction in his life. He was a strong and solidly built man. It was a privilege to be around him — just in the hopes that muscles were contagious!
>
> He told me of the time he was representing his country at the Olympics. It was a story of dreams that had struggled against a potential nightmare. From the age of twelve, the Olympics had been all he labored for. He had put every penny he earned and every purchase he made into someday becoming a gold medalist in the event he loved. He was totally focused. This is what he wanted. But he had a very turbulent relationship with his father, who had no interest in this dream of his, and therefore, he had funded every penny himself.

When he was only seventeen, he filmed the world champion in the event for which he was training and broke down his every stride, frame by frame, to study his technique. He then had himself filmed in the same distance and matched it, stride for stride. By precisely piecing together where he was losing his precious seconds to the world champion, he determined to bridge the gap. Through sheer willpower, discipline, and courage his goal was within reach. He made the cut for his country's team, and life was suddenly like being atop a floating cloud. He won every heat and was emerging as the surprise and potential winner when the finals came. Was this a dream or was it real? No, it was real, he reminded himself.

He was at the starting point for the finals, and his nation was watching. Millions were cheering for him, and hearts were racing, expecting this "country boy makes it big" story to hit the headlines the next day. In fact, I remember watching the event. The gun was about to go off, signaling the start. This was the moment he had waited for most of his life. But the mind with all its tenacity and resoluteness is also a storehouse of unuttered yearnings.

"From out of nowhere," he said, "an unexpected thought suddenly flooded my mind—I wonder if my father is watching me." That unanticipated thought momentarily overcame him and may have added a fraction of a second to his first two strides, robbing him of the gold. With great credit, he still won the bronze. The third fastest in the world is no mean accomplishment. Yet to him, the victory on the track lost its luster when measured against the deeper yearnings of life—the approval of the ones you love. Little did this Olympian know how my heart was beating as he shared this story with me. I understood him well.[14]

A Kiss: Yes, of Course I Love You

In the prodigal parable, the returning son was literally showered with kisses from a delighted father. The Greek of the text describes far more than a genteel peck on the cheek. It translates, "He kept on kissing him."

We all want to know if we are loved. That is the nagging question that gnaws away inside each and every one of us. This prevailing question mark is what fuels much or even most of the activity that we call life.

> The joint, as Fats Waller would have said, was jumping ... and during the last set, the saxophone player took off on a terrific solo. He was a kid from some insane place like Jersey City or Syracuse. But somewhere along the line he had discovered he could say it with a saxophone. He stood there, wide-legged ... filling his narrow chest, shivering in the rags of his twenty odd years, and screaming through the horn, "Do you love me?" "Do you love me?" "Do you love me?" And again, "Do you love me?" "Do you love me?" "Do you love me?" The same phrase unbearably, endlessly and variously repeated with all the force the kid had ... the question was terrible and real. The boy was blowing with his lungs and guts out of his own short past; and somewhere in the past in gutters and gang fights ... in the acrid room, behind marijuana or the needles, under the smell in the precinct basement, he had received a blow from which he would never recover, and this no one wanted to believe. Do you love me? Do you love me? Do you love me? The men on the stand stayed with him cool and at a little distance, adding and questioning. But each man knew that the boy was blowing for every one of them.[15]

Let us find ways to express our love to those who are returning, who acutely feel a sense of being unlovely and perhaps unlovable. Our love must not be merely hinted, implied, or assumed.

A Ring and a Robe

In the prodigal parable, the Father bestows upon his returning son the unexpected gift (and in the eyes of the elder brother, the *outrageous* gift) of the *stole*—the regal, "best" robe. Added to that was a signet ring, which some say is the symbol of authority restored. The ring was used to stamp legal documents. The family checkbook was being handed over to the very man who had squandered a good portion of the family wealth—an outrageous, risky act.

Certainly the gifts given were acting to restore dignity for a boy who had dived headfirst into depravity. When Craig came home, plagued by self-doubt and devastated by his ongoing failures, Steve and Sherri continually reminded him that he could succeed. They seized upon every small victory and used them to remind him that with God, he could make a great success of his life. If we communicate a sense that we've got a pessimistic eye on the returning prodigal, and that we believe it will only be awhile before they completely mess up again, they will be disheartened. The party we offer includes the gift of trust, of positive expectation mingled with realism for the journey ahead.

Sandals: Forgiveness Insisted Upon

Slaves never wore fine clothes, and a sign of their slavery was that they were never allowed to wear shoes in the house. Only family members could do such a thing. The prodigal's expectations were low — to return as a hired servant. In our own hearts, we are going to have to forgive many things, like the times we've been used and episodes of anger when we became whipping posts for unjustified rage.

Steve and Sherri were never invited to Craig's apartment, effectively excluded from his life. He discouraged them from meeting his friends, as if he was ashamed of his parents. On one rare occasion, a few of his pals came with him to the house. As they were leaving, Sherri heard one of them comment to Craig, "I don't know what you mean about your parents. They're not bad at all!" Sherri smiled and wondered how she and Steve had been painted. But forgiveness is not about holding an inquest to dig through every perceived act of wrong; it is freely, fabulously letting go of the grief that we feel. It is not about denying that any wrong was done or trying to forget it completely; there will be times when memories flood back and we are reminded of our hurt. But forgiveness is a huge force that is able to conquer the greatest evil, and the first person to benefit from forgiving is usually the forgiver. It's an extreme example, but consider this scene from a recent courtroom trial in South Africa:

> A frail black woman stands slowly to her feet. She is something over seventy years of age. Facing her from across the room are several white security police officers, one of whom, Mr. Van der Broek, has just been tried and found implicated in the murders of both the woman's son and her husband some years before. It was indeed Mr. Van der Broek, it has now been established, who had come to the woman's home a number of years back, taken her son, shot him at point-blank range and then burned the young man's body on a fire while he and his officer partied nearby.

Several years later, Van der Broek and his cohorts had returned to take away her husband as well. For many months she heard nothing of his whereabouts. Then, almost two years after her husband's disappearance, Van der Broek came back to fetch the woman herself. How vividly she remembers that evening, going down to a place beside a river where she was shown her husband, bound and beaten, but still strong in spirit, lying on a pile of wood. The last words she heard from his lips as the officers poured gasoline over his body and set him aflame were, "Father, forgive them."

And now the woman stands in the courtroom and listens to the confessions offered by Mr. Van der Broek. A member of South Africa's Truth and Reconciliation Commission turns to her and asks, "So what do you want? How should justice be done to this man who has so brutally destroyed your family?"

"I want three things," begins the old woman calmly, but confidently. "I want first to be taken to the place where my husband's body was burned so that I can gather up the dust and give his remains a decent burial."

She pauses, then continues. "My husband and son were my only family. I want, secondly, therefore, for Mr. Van der Broek to become my son. I would like for him to come twice a month to the ghetto and spend a day with me so that I can pour out on him whatever love I still have remaining within me."

"And finally," she says, "I want a third thing. I would like Mr. Van der Broek to know that I offer him my forgiveness because Jesus Christ died to forgive. This was also the wish of my husband. And so, I would kindly ask someone to come to my side and lead me across this courtroom so that I can take Mr. Van der Broek in my arms, embrace him and let him know that he is truly forgiven."

As the court assistants come to lead the elderly woman across the room, Mr. Van der Broek, overwhelmed by what he has just heard, faints. And as he does, those in the courtroom, friends, family, neighbours—all victims of decades of oppression and injustice—begin to sing, softly, but assuredly, "Amazing grace, how sweet the sound, that saved a wretch like me."[16]

Perhaps, like me, you feel dwarfed by the greatness displayed by that noble woman. Yet her story describes what can happen in any human heart as we open ourselves to the God of the impossible.

Barbecues and Bands: Fun and Normality

When the prodigal finally came home in the lovely story that Jesus told, his father ordered the fattened calf to be slain—not as a sacrifice, but for a celebration.

Don't rush a returning prodigal into a prayer meeting; sometimes those who welcome prodigals smother them with suffocating intensity. And don't allow them to find themselves in a situation where they have to start pretending about their ongoing struggles. The danger of evangelical culture is that we like success stories, and people who testify that they are home aren't supposed to sneak out for day trips to the far country. If we're not careful, the cover-up and pretense can begin all over again.

Tears at Chili's

Sherri and Steve had imagined a thousand times what a moment like this might look like. What would it look like for

Craig to begin to turn around and come back to God? Just thinking about it seemed like indulging in an impossible fantasy. Craig's lifestyle was evidence that he was marching resolutely away from faith; his was no casual drifting. A sensitive and intelligent young man, they knew that Craig had made his mind up and that, it seemed, was that. And besides, this had gone on for so very long—over seven years—with few glimmers of hope. Perhaps this was the way it would be—always. Still, they occasionally indulged the fantasy. Perhaps he would hit rock bottom and end up in the home of a Christian friend, who would thoughtfully allow him to pour his heart out—and point him back to God. Maybe he would wander into a church service somewhere and the preacher would have some special insight from heaven about Craig's situation. More than an on-target sermon, Steve had imagined a leader with a special direct word from God about Craig, and he would share it with authority. Craig, weeping, would rush up to the altar at the end of the service and would telephone his parents with the great news an hour later.

Perhaps Craig would have a dream that was both winsome and fearful. Images depicting the great love of God would flash across his mind all through the night, mingled with sobering vignettes that showed him what the consequences of his drug and alcohol abuse might be. Sweating and traumatized, he would wake up, immediately fall to his knees at the bedside, and weep his way back to God.

None of that happened.

It was a happy family lunch in Chili's restaurant. Craig had been home for a few days and it had gone well. Now the five of them were enjoying good food and good company, with lots of laughter and, for once, easy conversation. Sherri looked across the table and enjoyed the sight of Steve relishing a wonderful time with his children and wished that this moment would never pass. Over the seven long years there had been precious too few times like this, and she determined to relish every second. Craig was leaving that day and soon all this would be a happy memory.

She wanted to tell Craig just how much they had enjoyed his company. There was a pause in the laughter, and so she smiled, touched his hand, and said, "We're going to miss you when you're gone."

His reply took her breath away. "Mom, you won't have to miss me. I've made a decision. I'm going back to Phoenix to pick up my stuff, and I'm coming right back. I need to get my life straightened out. Mom . . . Dad . . . I want to come home." Craig looked around the table. There was stunned silence. Everyone's eyes were brimming over with tears. And then he broke down and began to cry too. Other diners must have wondered what on earth was happening over at the table in the corner as the whole family hugged and cried out loud. Craig really was coming home, and it was clear that, most importantly, he wanted to get his life back on track with God.

The Journey Continues

Later that day, Steve and Sherri reflected on the conversation at Chili's. They were amazed, grateful, and incredulous—did Craig really mean what he had said? Was this just another promise that would be unfulfilled—although he'd never given a glimmer of hope before in the long, dark years.

Craig did follow through. He went back to Phoenix just long enough to pick up his stuff and then came home. Eventually he recommitted his life to Christ—and there began a long journey that continues to this day, not only for him but surely for us all. None of us are finally "home" until the last day, when we will be out of reach of the Tempter's power.

Craig's was not a homecoming to a "happily ever after" existence, a restoration to an idyllic Christian life once more. There were times when he binged again and had to learn that a mistake is not the end. He constantly needed assurance and support. Some of his friendships continued to have a strong hold, and it was not until he went away for an intensive, residential training course that much of that hold was broken. His steps of homecoming to God didn't mean that all issues were resolved relationally, and it certainly wasn't the end of his questions. Steve and Sherri needed grace for when their son was in the far country, and grace too to keep the party of welcome going when he came home to God and to them.

Today, Craig's life is going in a very different direction than when he was a young man buffeted by addiction and anger. But perhaps we should let him speak for himself.

chapter ten

From Craig

When I was fourteen, I bumped into a brave, exciting new world—and I liked it very much. I found myself in what I'd been told was enemy territory. Rumor had it that I was in danger in that place that sounded both sinister and inviting. This was supposedly where bad people lingered and joy was in short supply. But as I dipped my toe into the murky waters normally tagged by church people as "the world," I was surprised. I liked the feeling, and I wanted more. And those "bad" people were also very nice—at least to me—and I wanted to be like them and be with them.

Church had been the center of my orbit up until then. My parents were involved in full-time Christian ministry and church had generally been a good experience for me. There were a few difficult seasons, like when we moved from our hometown of Pueblo. I thought my world would end as I waved good-bye to my lifelong friends. We relocated because my parents accepted another ministry position in Fort Collins, but to my surprise, the youth group there was strong; the youth pastor was fun, relevant, and caring; and I fit in well.

But my need to fit in was a sure step onto a pathway that very nearly destroyed me. In junior high school, I started hanging out with a bunch of guys who were great fun. We'd play pool, listen to rap music, and go for walks late into the night. I found myself desperately wanting to please my new crowd—they were the greatest. Little did I know that I would come to think of them—and others like them—as my new family. The family that had raised me, where I'd learned to speak and laugh, where my tears had been wiped away—*that* family would soon be shunted into the background.

"I Was Astride in Two Worlds"

Someone in our group decided to try drugs, and we all piled in for the experience. I was certain that this was a one-off or maybe something that I would do just a few times. I told myself that I was the master of my own destiny, and that I wouldn't be bitten by the deadly toxins of addiction. I was very wrong. The drug use accelerated at an alarming rate.

Meanwhile, I was still a part of the church youth group, but a disorienting sense of schizophrenia was setting in. I was astride in two worlds that were totally incompatible—more than that, they were at war with each other. On one hand, I felt like I could juggle my way between the two, but then the conflict threw up huge questions about God that I just didn't have the will or energy to face. Suddenly, I wasn't sure what Christianity was all about—was God the one who propped up some of the meaningless religious traditions that didn't make any sense to me? I couldn't answer that question or separate Christ from the confusing fog that was Christianity —but, at the same time, what was very solid and dependable was the commitment of my friends. They were there for me in the here and now. God and the hereafter seemed a very long way away. I didn't abandon my faith, but just filed it away as pending. Now my preoccupation was with the next party and the next high. I spent even more time with my friends. We would defend each other to the point of violence.

Soon my new world became my main world, with occasional dips back into religion. Church was a place for Sunday mornings and Wednesday nights, but in truth, I couldn't wait for the service to be over so I could get on with my real life. And I found other members of the youth group who were playing the same game I was, smoking dope in the church parking lot and then popping into the church building for a vague "dose" of God (or rather, watching others get a dose of him). Then, when the service ended, they rushed out to do what was really important and attractive.

There's no such thing as level ground when you're doing your best to ignore God; you find yourself on a downhill slope. I graduated to drugs of greater potency; after all, I trusted my friends implicitly—literally, with my life. If they were doing that stuff, I was happy to walk the pathway they had trodden. But the grip of substance and alcohol abuse was subtly tightening around me. My insistence that I was in control was ringing hollow in my own ears.

My Group Was My God

Inevitably, my parents found drugs in my room, and there were huge blowouts—without any resolution. My response to them was simple: it's my life, and I'm okay with this. I probably won't understand what pain I caused them until I have children of my own. By now, my school attendance had very little to do with education. It was just a place to hang out. My group was now my god. My cocktail of drug use included LSD, cocaine, ecstasy, and methamphetamine— often followed by an alcohol chaser or two. Or ten.

It was time for me to move out from the family home, allegedly to get my own space. There wasn't much space to be had; most nights there were at least twenty or thirty people hanging around our downtown apartment, and sometimes as many as two or three hundred came through. I lived in almost unending chaos. The police were frequent visitors too, such was our reputation.

My family would drive by to see me, but I never felt able to invite them inside to see my home. Sometimes the sight of the motley crew hanging out on our porch would be too much for them. There were times when I peered through the drapes and saw my sisters just sitting in the car, staring at our house of madness. They were in tears. Soon cards and letters from my sisters arrived, begging me to consider the way my life was going and affirming how much they loved and missed me. Sometimes their words would reduce me to tears, and for a while, in the isolation of my room, I'd weep. But then pride would engulf me once more, and I'd tell myself that they were naïve church kids, that they didn't understand my big, bad, sophisticated world.

Eager to pursue my dreams in music, I moved to Phoenix and became lead singer in a band. With my new career hopes I decided to try to kick the drugs, but used more and more alcohol as a substitute. I would drink until I blacked out, often finishing off an eighteen-pack of beer solo. My sleep patterns were totally erratic; often I'd be up until four a.m., so not only was the booze taking its effect, but I was permanently sleep-deprived too.

The band was going well, so we made plans to relocate yet again, this time to San Diego to hit the music scene there. But just before the move, I went home for Christmas. While I was there, I suddenly realized that I was completely unhappy. My life was a hollow sham without direction or fulfillment. In a conversation with one of my sisters, I said that I didn't know if I could carry on living like this. Her reply, so simple and direct, hit me like a stun grenade.

"You don't have to." In a moment, I realized that I could take hold of the reins of my existence once more; that I didn't have to drift, place my life in the hands of my friends, or suspend action indefinitely. This was not an instant turnaround, but the beginning of a long, hard journey home to God. It was not a strong, resolute march back to get in step with him, but the tiny beginnings of a journey that continues to this very day. That night, I ate at Chili's with my family, and my mom told me that she was going to miss me. I remember replying that she wouldn't have to miss me, because I'd decided to come back and get my life sorted out. We all cried with relief. It sounded so easy. My parents had known pain while I was away. Getting me back on the right pathway was to usher in a different kind of pain, where their ability to maintain hope and help pray me through would be every bit as necessary as in the previous phase of the journey.

But I did follow through in coming home — immediately. I went back to Phoenix, packed up all my stuff, and nervously approached my friends to tell them of my decision. I was expecting a fistfight, because my leaving to go home would seriously affect the destiny of the other members of the band. Remarkably, they were cool with my choice. I drove home, hopes high.

It was really difficult. I was trying to get things sorted out, but back home there was a network of old relationships ready and waiting for me. I was arrested a number of times, charged with assault and disorderly conduct. I had a fake

ID that allowed me to still drink heavily. But I was slowly beginning to face up to the harsh reality that I did have a serious problem with alcohol.

During that difficult time, there were three episodes that made a significant impact upon me. The first was meeting an old drinking buddy at a party. He told me about how he'd become a Christian and how his life had and was being totally changed. I looked into his eyes and saw something very genuine there—and I was really pleased for him, grateful that his choice was working out for him. Prodigals don't all spit on religion—it's just that sometimes they don't have the will to embrace it for themselves.

And then I met another Christian in a bar. At first, I thought that he must be a Buddhist—I'd been told that he was religious—but there he was, drinking a beer with us and being so warm, so normal. We had a thirty-second conversation in the restroom, during which he told me that he had studied many religions. And then he said, with simplicity and power, "I have decided to follow Jesus Christ." Those simple words hit me like a slap on the side of the head.

The third incident happened during a church service. One of my sisters was singing and I'd decided to go along and listen to her. It was as if those who had planned the service knew that I was coming (which they didn't) and had set up every moment, every word, and designed them to have the maximum impact upon me.

That night, years of pride were broken as I walked to the front of the church to publicly confess my allegiance to Jesus Christ: I wanted to follow him myself now, like the guy I'd chatted with in the bathroom. I will never forget that night. My prayer of commitment and repentance was muddled, yet somehow surely heard. I told God that I wanted to live for him, but that I had no idea how to do that. What happened in the ensuing months demonstrated just how confused I was—and how faithful and patient he is.

I went to different churches so as not to be tagged as the returning prodigal. My battle with alcohol continued, but there was something new at the center of me, struggling to emerge even in my darkest times. I can remember sharing my faith in Jesus in bars when I was completely drunk.

I Had to Escape My Network

Finally I realized that I had to escape the demands of my Fort Collins social network. I planned to go to Youth With A Mission in Honolulu, but even in the few days before I left, the battle heated up. I was grieving for the loss of my second family, my drinking pals. Just before I left, I was arrested again. I sat in the cell and prayed a predictable but heartfelt prayer: "Here I am again. Help me." I pleaded with the judge to let me go to YWAM. He gave me a sentence that included community service, hoping perhaps that YWAM would give me a new start.

My first day there was turbulent, as other newcomers to the program shared their testimonies. Most of them were bright-eyed, keen eighteen- or nineteen-year-olds. I was now a twenty-two-year-old drunk, had no idea where I was going, and when it came time for me to speak, I cried like a baby for ten minutes.

After that trip, I went to Indonesia for three months, had a wonderful time, and returned to Fort Collins on a spiritual high, imagining myself to be ready to face and indeed bring transformation to my home scene. My enthusiasm lasted a few weeks. Soon I was back in the chaos of binging again.

Now I realized that I needed to seriously break the patterns in my life. If I was to be a Christian, I needed to give myself to a sustained period of discipleship training. I went back to YWAM and this time was posted to Kurdistan for eighteen months. That was such a turning point for me. Now I meant business. That didn't signal an ending to the struggles and sins—but the lessons learned in the tough boot-camp atmosphere of Kurdistan were invaluable.

When it came time for me to come back to Colorado, my former youth pastor, who had now moved to lead a church himself, invited me to become full-time worship pastor for the alternative service that he was starting. I accepted the role, which has been a fantastic experience. I continue in that position today, although I think that something new is brewing. I'm aware of my vulnerabilities still, but at ease about my future. God really has steered me through some storms. I don't believe too much in me, but I do believe in him in me.

This is not one of those happily-ever-after stories. Of course I fall, and I have to get back up—just like us all. The journey never ends this side of death. There are still moments of real shame and conviction, but they are coupled with a determination to push through and just keep going. I've also learned I don't want to become a pleaser of my new crowd, the church people. I want to keep asking those awkward questions about why we do what we do. Coming home for me does not mean silent acquiescence to everything that goes on in God's name. Compliance has gotten me into too much trouble. I don't want to embrace a new, "saintly" compliance and drift into a vague, bland faith that will not ultimately affect my world or sustain me.

Looking back, I'm so grateful that through those dark years my parents listened, loved, watched, and talked. I know that they still pray for me daily. The dangers that I face are different now, but they are dangers nonetheless.

If you love a prodigal, never give up. Be real. Be prepared to share what a life lived for God really means. And when you do pray for a prodigal to come home to God, question your own motives. Why do you want them back? Is it for them, or for you? Perhaps it is for both of you.

I'm told that when things were at their bleakest, my parents made a decision that they would love me unconditionally until I died, or they died, whatever came first. Their love for me would not be dependent on where I was or how I lived; it was nonnegotiable.

I'm so thankful for that, so thankful for them.

I'm pushing through with Jesus. Today is another day.

chapter eleven

A Parting Word

*O*ur time together is almost done. I sincerely hope that the words we have shared together have given you a sense of authentic hope, a conviction that, although you often feel lonely, you are not alone. I trust that heavy weights of guilt might have been lifted from your weary shoulders, and that your praying has been helped as you continue across the battlefield that is life. Perhaps you have found that your prodigal is no prodigal at all. I hope we've thought again about what "coming home" means, and that we've faced the reality that all good parties call for sacrifice, expense—and a mess to clean up. May Craig's journey inspire us. He is a wonderful, flawed, passionate, restless disciple of Jesus to this day. I am honored to know him and to count Steve and Sherri among my friends.

In writing this book, I was profoundly moved by the story of the lady who always leaves the light on for her son, despite it being so many years since she has seen him. I think of her often. What must it feel like to walk into that silent room every night without fail, to end another day with a glimmer of hopefulness that flies in the face of twenty-five years of silence? Somewhere out there is her beloved son, and so still she climbs the stairs to do something for him, something that he may never know about, but that is an act of faithful love nonetheless. What does she feel as she fumbles for that light switch for the seven-thousandth time? Surely, however long her son is away, she hopes that one day his eye might fall upon that light—that even though the distance between them has been compounded by the years, that tomorrow could be a better, brighter day. I think that, if need be—and may it not be necessary—she will climb those stairs until her dying day.

Whoever the prodigals are in your life, whatever their specific circumstances, and wherever in the world they are at this moment, let's agree together, now and always: we'll always leave the light on.

Do you love someone who is apparently walking in a "prodigal" lifestyle? Please visit *www.jefflucas.org/ prodigals* for books, teaching resources, news of prayer events and conferences, and for the opportunity to be part of an emerging prayer network. The website also carries an excerpt from Jeff Lucas's forthcoming book on *The Prodigal-Friendly Church.*

Prodigal Blessing

May you always know
where the road home begins
and have the courage to walk the first mile.
May you never be too far from a lifeline
and never too far gone to dial.

May you know
that the God who pursues you
is a hunter whose bullets bleed mercy.
May artful accidents of grace
explode at every turn of your journey.

May you trip over truth
and fall headlong into hope.
May redemption rain down all around you.
May God's glory catch you napping
and God's story catch your breath
and God's gratuity perpetually astound you.

May choices you thought you'd made at random
turn out to be the key to moving on.
May the darkness that sometimes surrounds you
prove to be the moment before dawn.

May you bathe in the light
of a prodigal sun
and be nourished
by a generous earth.
May the struggles you meet
make you stronger
and even old wounds bring new wonders to birth.

May you trip over truth
and fall headlong into hope.
May redemption rain down all around you.
May God's glory catch you napping
and God's story catch your breath
and God's gratuity perpetually astound you.

May the unplanned kindnesses of strangers
bring to mind a long-forgotten song.
May the unexpected kisses
of a star-filled sky
remind you of where you belong.

And even if you never return to find peace
amongst those who have so loved and so hurt you,
may you seek your soul's redeemer
and connect with your creator
and make your home
with the Father who waits for you.

May you trip over truth
and fall headlong into hope.
May redemption rain down all around you.
May God's glory catch you napping
and God's story catch your breath
and God's gratuity perpetually astound you.

GERARD KELLY

Notes

CHAPTER ONE

A Familiar Story

1. Isaiah 53:6
2. Matthew 8:28–34
3. Philip Richter and Leslie Francis, *Gone but Not Forgotten: Church Leaving and Returning* (London: Darton, Longman and Todd, 1998).

CHAPTER TWO

Cruel School

1. John 16:33
2. C. S. Lewis, *The Four Loves* (San Diego: Harvest Books, 1971).
3. Quoted in M. Volf, *Exclusion and Embrace: Theological Reflections in the Wake of Ethnic Cleansing* (Nashville: Abingdon, 1996); W. Dyrness, ed., *Emerging Voices in Global Christian Theology* (Grand Rapids, Mich.: Zondervan, 1994).
4. Rob Parsons, *Bringing Home the Prodigals* (London: Hodder and Stoughton, 2003), 18.
5. Margie M. Lewis, *The Hurting Parent* (Grand Rapids, Mich.: Zondervan, 1980), 81, 83.

6. C. S. Lewis, *The Problem of Pain* (New York: Macmillan, 1962), 40–41.
7. Rob Parsons, *Bringing Home the Prodigals.*
8. Romans 5:3–4
9. 1 Peter 4:13
10. Aleksandr I. Solzhenitsyn, *The Gulag Archipelago: 1918–1956* (New York: Harper, 2002).

CHAPTER THREE

Who Are the Prodigals?

1. Luke 2:41–50
2. Luke 5:30
3. Luke 7:32
4. Luke 11:15
5. Mark 3:20–21
6. John 14:31
7. Walter Bruggemann, *Biblical Perspectives on Evangelism: Living in a Three-Storied Universe* (Nashville: Abingdon, 1993).
8. Simon Jones, *Why Bother with Church?* (Downers Grove, Ill.: InterVarsity, 2001), 29.
9. Steve Chalke, *Intelligent Church* (Grand Rapids, Mich.: Zondervan, 2006).

10. 2 Corinthians 6:17
11. Matthew 23:1–39 is hardly an exercise in subtlety!
12. Galatians 5:12
13. Tony Campolo, *Seven Deadly Sins* (Colorado Springs: Victor Books, 1987), 23.
14. John Killinger, "When We Stop Being Free," *Pulpit Digest*, July/August 1992, 12–13.
15. Romans 7:21–24
16. Matthew 18:6
17. Marshall Shelley, *The Healthy Hectic Home: Raising a Family in the Midst of Ministry* (Christianity Today; Word Pub.; Distributed by Word Books: Carol Stream, Ill.; Dallas, 1988).

CHAPTER FOUR

God Knows

1. Hosea 11:3
2. Mark Stibbe, *From Orphans to Heirs: Celebrating Our Spiritual Adoption* (Oxford: BRF, 1999).
3. "'Does God Suffer?' Interview with Nicholas P. Wolterstorff," *Modern Reformation* (Sept./Oct. 1999), 45.
4. Exodus 3:7
5. Psalm 31:7
6. Matthew 14:36
7. Jeremiah 14:17
8. Hosea 11:8
9. Isaiah 42:5–8
10. Mark 11:17
11. Genesis 39:2
12. Exodus 2:23

CHAPTER FIVE

Reasons for Hope

1. Proverbs 22:6
2. Proverbs 3:10
3. Rob Parsons, *Bringing Home the Prodigals* (London: Hodder and Stoughton, 2003), 3.
4. Jonah 1:3
5. Luke 24:13ff
6. Henri Nouwen, *The Return of the Prodigal Son* (New York: Doubleday, 1992), 82.
7. James 5:17
8. 1 Kings 19:1–18
9. Henri Nouwen, *Return of the Prodigal Son*, 106–7.
10. Excerpted from Francis Thompson, "The Hound of Heaven."
11. Georges Bernanos, *The Diary of a Country Priest* (New York: Carroll and Graf, 2002).
12. Jeff Lucas, *How Not to Pray* (Carlisle: Spring Harvest, 2002).
13. John 20:15
14. Tom Bisset, *Why Christian Kids Leave the Faith* (Grand Rapids, Mich.: Discovery House, 1992), 206.
15. Michael Lloyd, *Cafe Theology* (London: Alpha International, 2005), 156.
16. Edith Deen, *Great Women of the Christian Faith* (Ulrichsville, Ohio: Barbour, 1959), 23.

CHAPTER SIX

Home Is?

1. Matthew 7:13–14
2. Rob Parsons, *Bringing Home the Prodigals* (London: Hodder and Stoughton, 2003).
3. Lesslie Newbigin, Sanneh, and Taylor, *Faith*, quoted in Steve Chalke, *One God* (Uchfield: Spring Harvest Publishing, 2006).

4. M. Volf, *Exclusion and Embrace: Theological Reflections in the Wake of Ethnic Cleansing* (Nashville: Abingdon, 1996).
5. 1 Samuel 15:23 KJV
6. Dave Andrews and Tim Costello, *Christianarchy: Discovering a Radical Spirituality of Compassion* (Oxford: Lion Hudson, 1999).
7. Donald W. McCullough, *The Trivialization of God* (Colorado Springs: NavPress, 1995), 36.
8. Matthew 19:13
9. Matthew 17:4
10. John 18:10
11. Mark 6:36
12. Matthew 16:22
13. Carolyn Ros, *Broken Dreams, Fulfilled Promises* (Eastbourne: Kingsway, 2006), 16.

CHAPTER SEVEN

Guilty as Charged?

1. Matthew 7:11, italics mine
2. Psalm 145:4
3. Rob Parsons, *Bringing Home the Prodigals* (London: Hodder and Stoughton, 2003).
4. Ann Landers, *The Ann Landers Encyclopedia: A to Z* (New York: Doubleday, 1978), 514–17.
5. Wayne Dyer, *Your Erroneous Zones* (New York: Avon, 2001).
6. Matthew 5:48
7. Rob Parsons, *Bringing Home the Prodigals*.
8. Adapted from Steve Chalke, *He Never Said: Discover the Real Message of Jesus* (London: Hodder and Stoughton, 2000).
9. Rob Parsons, *Bringing Home the Prodigals*.

10. Marshall Shelley, *The Healthy Hectic Home: Raising a Family in the Midst of Ministry* (Christianity Today; Word Pub.: Distributed by Word Books: Carol Stream, Ill.; Dallas, 1988).
11. Rob Parsons, *Bringing Home the Prodigals*.

CHAPTER EIGHT

Praying for the Prodigals

1. 1 Samuel 1:10
2. Quoted in Parsons, *Bringing Home the Prodigals* (London: Hodder and Stoughton, 2003), 17.
3. Mark 12:40
4. Quinn Sheerer and RuthAnne Garlock, *Praying the Prodigals Home* (Ventura, Calif.: Regal Books, 2000), 53.
5. Luke 18:1
6. James 4:3
7. Robert Farrer Capon, *The Parables of Grace* (Grand Rapids, Mich.: Eerdmans, 1996).
8. Genesis 32:26
9. Carol Kent, *Secret Longings of the Heart* (Colorado Springs: NavPress, 1990).
10. Luke 18:9–14
11. K. W. Osbeck, *Amazing Grace: 366 Inspiring Hymn Stories for Daily Devotions* (Grand Rapids, Mich.: Kregel, 1990).
12. 1 Corinthians 15:33
13. 2 Peter 3:17
14. 1 Kings 11:4
15. 1 Kings 12:13–14
16. Psalm 101:4–7
17. Acts 9:27
18. 2 Corinthians 4:4
19. Matthew 27:3
20. 2 Corinthians 7:9–10

21. Luke 22:31

22. Luke 4:1–13

23. John 12:2

CHAPTER NINE

Preparing the Party

1. Deuteronomy 14:25–26
2. Zephaniah 3:17
3. Luke 15:10
4. Luke 15:5–6
5. Luke 15:9
6. Matthew 22:14
7. Luke 7:34
8. Revelation 19:9
9. Jacob Neusner, *From Politics to Piety: The Emergence of Pharisaic Judaism* (Upper Saddle River, N.J.: Prentice-Hall, 1979), 80.
10. Matthew 15:1–3
11. Luke 10:33, 37
12. Luke 15:20
13. Matthew 9:13; 12:7; Hosea 6:6
14. Ravi Zacharias, *Jesus among Other Gods* (Nashville: W Publishing, 2002).
15. Donald W. McCullough, *The Trivialization of God* (Colorado Springs: NavPress, 1995).
16. James Kraybill, in *Keep the Faith, Share the Peace*, the newsletter of the Mennonite Church Peace and Justice Committee 5, no. 3 (June 1999).